JUSTICE AND LAW

Edited by

Steven P. Scalet

Volume II in the Series Philosophy, Politics, and Law
Global Academic Publishing, Binghamton University
Binghamton, New York
2009

SERIES IN PHILOSOPHY, POLITICS, AND LAW
Editor in Chief: Steven P. Scalet

Library of Congress Cataloging-in-Publication Data:

ISBN 978-1-58684-272-7

Justice and law / edited by Steven P. Scalet.
p. cm. -- (Series philosophy, politics, and law ; v. 2)
Includes bibliographical references.
ISBN 978-1-58684-272-7 (pbk. : alk. paper) 1. Law--United States--Philosophy. I. Scalet, Steven.
KF380.J87 2009
347.73'12--dc22

2008055434

Cover photograph by Steven P. Scalet
Cover design by Matthew J. Tynan

Published by:
Global Academic Publishing, Binghamton University
State University of New York
Binghamton, New York, USA 13902-6000
Phone: (607) 777-4495 Fax (607) 777-6132
E-mail: gap@binghamton.edu
http://academicpublishing.binghamton.edu/

PREFACE

How can a large public university offer its best undergraduate students both a small liberal arts and graduate-level experience within its undergraduate curriculum? This publication offers one answer to that question. Let top students apply for admission into a competitive honors program; inform them from the outset that at the end of their work a panel of academics will examine and judge their papers before a general conference audience; direct the writing process, encourage regular meetings and debates among the honors students, and coach them on delivering a scholarly paper. These were the basic ingredients that led to this publication. Each of the papers is an original work by the student author, both in conception and development.

This book is the second volume in the *Series in Philosophy, Politics, and Law*. Topics range over any area of philosophy. The title of the series recognizes the role of Binghamton University's Program in Philosophy, Politics, and Law (PPL) in creating the series. PPL includes core courses in philosophy and complimentary courses in history, political science, economics, and other humanities and social sciences, ending in a B.A. degree in Philosophy, Politics, and Law. PPL is one of the most popular majors on campus, sending more students to law school than any other major at Binghamton University. PPL offers its majors a strong liberal arts education, and the Pell Honors Program is part of creating the personal attention that is the hallmark of small liberal arts colleges.

Each paper has its own abstract so there is no need to repeat those summarizes here. The title *Justice and Law* conveys the fact that all of these papers discuss controversial topics at the intersection of justice and law.

It is with great pleasure that I recognize the people who have made this project possible. Above all, I wish to thank alumnus Owen C. Pell, Esq. '80, whose financial and intellectual contributions made possible the organization of these proceedings. Mr. Pell has devoted his energy and enthusiasm for liberal arts education at Binghamton University. He has been a frequent guest lecturer to the classroom and other public events at Binghamton University, and his captivating speaking style and command over a vast range of issues in law and legal philosophy make him a favorite among students. It is an honor to give him tribute. Owen Pell exemplifies the values of life-long learning in his own life and is a model for young undergraduate students. The Pell Honors Program is named to recognize his legacy and formative contributions.

I am also grateful to the late Professor John Arthur whose dedication and work as the previous director of PPL created great vibrancy for the PPL Program. There was no program idea too small or too large that John would not consider supporting, including this honors program, and always with devotion to his undergraduate students. I would also like to thank the philosophy department at Binghamton University for supporting the mission of the Pell Honors Program and Lori Fuller at Global Academic Publications for her editorial assistance in creating this publication.

Steven P. Scalet
Director, Program in Philosophy, Politics, and Law
Associate Professor, Philosophy and Economics

CONTENTS

JUSTICE AND LAW

Abstract

This paper will attempt to uncover the social structures that account for the continuation of the sexual violence against women, as well as define the ironic moral attachment that society has placed on the crime of rape as it continues to perpetuate its occurrence.

It will further show the paradoxical relationship between the social conditions which continue to exist in American culture, and the legal considerations implicated by the crime of rape.

RAPE, SLAVERY, AND INJUSTICE FOR ALL

Stephanie A. Dodge

Introduction

As students at Binghamton University arrive on campus to begin their college careers, they each receive a packet titled, "Rape and Sexual Assault: What You Should Know." Rape and other types of sexual violence are topics of grave concern in American society, and determining how to combat those crimes stirs debate within the legal profession.

The "National Violence Against Women Survey," taken in 2002 by the National Institute of Justice, estimates that 17.6% of women in the United States have survived a completed or attempted rape (Tjaden & Nancy Thoennes 2000). One in six women will become a victim of some type of sexual violence in their lifetimes, and college age women are four times more likely to be victimized (RAINN 2008). In 2006, it was estimated that someone is sexually assaulted every two minutes in the United States, and women are more than five times more likely then men to be the victims (ibid.). In fact, in 2005, 92% of sexual assault victims were female (National Center for Victims of Crime, 2008). These statistics are devastating; sexual crimes are targeting women, and doing so frequently and violently. Yet, before this pervasive problem can be resolved, it is essential to examine how and why is occurs.

American society presents an interesting duality in regards to sexual violence. Social conditions within society are responsible for perpetuating the occurance of such violence, yet this same society has ironically placed great moral and legal significance on sexual crimes. While society creates an atmosphere wrought with sexual violence, it frowns upon its occurrence and has crafted its legal system to comport with this disapproving view. Thus, an unavoidable paradox is created within social life in which society simultaneously fosters and opposes sexual crimes.

Social Conditions Behind the Crime of Rape

Beneath the Surface

Within each society there are underlying assumptions upon which social and legal structures are built. It is these assumptions that guide members of that society in learning to interact and relate to one another (Bartett 1990: 829–888).

For example, the boldly declared words, "all men are created equal," resounding in the echo of the Declaration of Independence, were not always interpreted as they are today. This banner of freedom and equality was uttered in a time when society held fast to an underlying assumption that black males did not legally constitute men. Therefore, the seemingly race-neutral and liberating language of "all men are created equal," was not neutral in practice as it was not applied to males of all races.

Though perhaps not as painfully obvious as creating a class of "submen," there continues to exist underlying assumptions and hidden social structures regarding women that perpetuate an unconscious stereotyping, and shapes how they are viewed and treated within society. Due to the fact that the American social and legal systems were founded and maintained by a male-dominated society, such stereotyping became embedded into the social fabric.[1] While living in such a society, people learn to accept imbalances between the genders and even become blind to their existence. Social structures have become so engrained into American cultural life that they are now accepted as the norm (ibid.).

The subordination of women may no longer be forwardly declared as the proper role of women in society as has been done in the past, but repercussions of this former role have had lasting effects on how women are viewed today. The subordination of women has left the face of social life and buried itself beneath the surface.

The fact that the crime of rape exists at all, especially as prevalent as it is today, is evidence that an underlying assumption of women's inferior position in society still exists. Rape is a crime of power; when a man rapes a woman he is taking away all forms of her personal governance (Cochran 2008). In a sense, he is stripping her of her ability to act as an autonomous human being. If women were truly considered equal to their male counterparts, such a degrading violation would not exist.

Further, the fact that women are targeted as victims show that rape is not merely a crime of sexual impulse between heterosexuals, as it does not affect both genders equally. This reveals a social relationship between the genders.

Consider, for instance, a male prison society. In such a society, the inmates create a hierarchy amongst themselves. They divide themselves into various groups where some are considered superior to others based on the power they wield. It is known amongst the inmates that they are not all considered equal. It is those who are considered weaker, and thus inferior, who become the victims of rape in that society (Anderson 2004: 4).[2] This social phenomenon evidences that it is an "inferior" group that is targeted for sexual crimes. In America's free society, an estimated 91% of victims of rape are female, and 99% of offenders are male (UCSC 1999). Clearly, it is women who are the victimized group, the perceived "inferior" group. As one can see from the male inmates in the prison hierarchy, victimization is not based on inherent qualities within the female gender, but rather a hierarchical system that is casting certain groups into an inferior role.

If the two genders were considered equal, the crime of rape, which forces women into a submissive role, would not occur nearly as frequently as it does. As we continue to live in a society with undertones of women's inferiority, we are conditioned to accept preconceived notions regarding women and perpetuate patterns of behavior that comport with such views. The cycle will not end if we do not recognize the underlying assumptions with which we live.

Sex Sells: Sexualizing Society's View of Women

In American society, women are constantly portrayed as sexual objects. Television commercials feature women selling various products such as liquor, cars or soft drinks while wearing revealing clothing and sexually appealing makeup. After all, the old motto goes, "sex sells." It becomes obvious why women are seen as sexual objects when society continues to present them in this manner.

However, it is not just the media that perpetuates a sexualized view of women; it is women themselves. Short skirts, form fitting clothing, and high heels are normal attire for today's woman. But one must ask why this is the norm. One may believe that these things look nice and women like to wear them; and while this is often the case, it does not explain why women like to wear such items or how they became fashionable.

Women's fashions are designed to appeal to men. Women's clothing is often tighter and more revealing than men's, highlighting their forms and accenting gender-specific features. In this way, women dress to appeal to men even while they may not realize it. The things we like or desire are shaped by the society we live in, as conceptions of the good are determined by our collective social values and opinions (Westermark 2006: 66). Thus, it is not surprising that in a society that was once dominated by men, it has become accepted that women's clothing should be appealing to men. At one time, women had a need to attract men as they relied on them for income and social acceptance. While this is no longer the case, with women's independent role in modern society, women's clothing has continued through the years to appeal to the opposite sex in a way that men's clothing never had to. In some sense, it may be a relic of the outdated social value that a woman was expected to find a husband to support her.

The sexualization of women is perpetuated and reproduced daily as the media continues to show women in a sexual light, and women continue to embrace fashions that are designed to attract men. It is a personal choice for each woman as to whether or not she will continue to follow such social norms; however, in order to make an informed decision, it is essential to recognize why these norms exist as they do.

Unrecognized conceptions of women as sexual objects can be horrifyingly dangerous for society. On May 9, 2006, the Associated Press printed a story of twelve young boys in the first and second grade who were accused of sexually assaulting a second grade girl at recess (Associated Press 2006). One must question how these children came to view females as sexual objects, and why the boys felt it acceptable to force a classmate into a submissive and sexual role.

When women are conditioned to act and dress in such a way that is crafted to appeal to men, it perpetuates an implication that women are inferior to men. This subliminal casting of women as the inferior gender is being so clearly depicted throughout society that boys the age of eight years old have come to accept it as the norm. The children in the article in the Associated Press saw a female classmate not as an equal, but as a sexual object that they could force into a submissive role long before natural sexual feelings occurred to them.

Social structures within society cast women as an inferior and sexualized gender, making them the obvious target for sexual violence. Notwithstanding the existence of these structures which perpetuate such crimes, society has ironically woven a great amount of morality into to the very word "rape."

Morally Laced

The Word "Rape"

Upon hearing the mere utterance of the word "rape," there is instilled in many people a moral torrent of unease and displeasure. The single word carries with it a great amount of morality. In this way, it can be said that "rape" is a morally laced term; meaning, it is a word that can not be defined by a common dictionary definition. The moral sentiment attached to the word is so deeply entwined in society's understanding of it, that the true essence of the word can not be revealed void of that morality. Such morally laced terms incite an immediate reaction amongst those who grasp its full meaning.

For example, a dictionary defines rape as, "any act of sexual intercourse that is forced upon a person" (Dictionary.com 2008). The New York Penal Code defines the crime of rape in the first degree as "engag[ing] in sexual intercourse with another person by forcible compulsion" (NY PENAL §130.35). However displeasing such definitions sound, they do not explain the moral unrest caused by the mention of the act.

Defining the Morally Laced

There are several aspects to the crime of rape that make it stand out as morally repugnant in the minds of many. Unlike other crimes, such as assault, rape carries with it the following characteristics that invoke sentiments of morality at the mention of the word.[3]

FORCE AND COERCION

The first element, which may strike one as obvious, is the use of force or coercion, which is a necessary component of rape. When a victim is forced to submit to sexual acts it removes her sense of autonomy. The victim loses all control over a situation involving her own body; there is a complete loss of independence and self-governance, and value of the individual is compromised by such a loss.

The American legal system preaches equality amongst all individuals, as each person is considered equally valuable (Locke 1690: 342). To remove a person's sense of autonomy through forced submission is to disregard the victim's value as a human being. In a country that holds the worth of the individual in such high regards, a forced crime, such as rape, seems morally incompatible with the over-lying value systems of autonomy and self-worth.

Coercion weighs equally with force in the sense that victims so severely fear the consequences of defending themselves from the rape that they have little choice but to allow it to occur. In the same way that a physically forced victim could not escape her fate, a coerced victim feels that she too has no realistic options.[4]

It should be an individual's choice as to whether or not she wishes to engage in sexual acts and with whom she wishes to engage in those acts; the rape victim is stripped of those choices through force or coercion.

VICTIMIZATION ON THE BASIS OF GENDER

Victimization of the basis of gender is a second component responsible for the moral sentiments aroused by the crime of rape.

The fact that women are more than five times more likely than men to be the victim of rape creates a certain level of unrest (RAINN 2008). If rape did not affect one gender as opposed to the other, the crime would lose its shock value. Of course, the rape of a woman and the rape of a man are equally traumatic, but if rape was a problem that consistently affected both genders, some of the moral ties to the crime would be lost.

This is because rape is a crime of power in which the victim looses control and the attacker assumes it (Cochran 2008). Women, who have historically been seen as the physically weaker gender, appear to be easy prey for rapists.[5] The female gender is targeted for its perceived vulnerability. The idea of one person assuming control over another who is not expected to fend off the attack seems both unfair and immoral. Regardless of whether or not the victim is capable of warding off her attacker, the rapist had intended to overpower, by force or coercion, a person whom they had perceived to be physically inferior.

The idea of the defenseless women is often highlighted and perpetuated in society. For example, young boys are often taught not to hit girls. This message carries with it many underlying implications. It implies that it is wrong to hit another person when that person is weaker, and not that it is simply wrong to harm another person.

While it must be recognized that women are often physically weaker then men, women can still be recognized as an equal gender while acknowledging and respecting the limitations and capabilities of both genders. Rapists fail to recognize such equality as they victimize based on gender and the physical vulnerability they perceive the female gender to encompass.

SEXUAL NATURE

A third component to the moral ties attached to rape is the sexual nature of the crime.

Sexuality is a subject that is in many ways regulated and controlled. Consider, for instance, the institution of marriage. What began as a religious notion has taken on new secular purposes.

Historically, marriage was intended as a control on sexuality, and in many religions it limits sexual encounters to one partner (Hyams 2006). To do otherwise was harshly frowned upon and seen as immoral.[6] Many major religions view intercourse as important in some way, and therefore encourage certain forms of regulation (Doniger 2007). If sexuality was not a major moral concern, this type of consistency, even amongst otherwise conflicting religions, would not arise.

As marriage and intercourse have become topics of secular concern, the government has harnessed the controls that religion once imposed on society. Sexuality remains an area that is, to a significant extent, controlled and regulated. Though sexuality is now less taboo than it has been in the past, society has been trained to see it as topic that is significant in nature due to the fact that it has been closely controlled by both religion and government for centuries (ibid.). Therefore, crimes, such as rape, that target sexuality are considered especially heinous and invoke sentiments of morality, as it is interpreted as a violation of an important, personal subject matter.

VIOLATION OF THE BODY

Rape is not only a violation against sexuality, but it is a violation of the victim's body.

Preceding societal laws, human beings carried the instinctual, overwhelming desire to protect their own lives and well-beings. In this way, the body is the core sense of property, and people will desire to protect this property from what they sense is harmful or undesirable.[7] A rapist claims the body of another person as their own property; property that the rapist can control and use at his own discretion. Essentially, rape forces the victim to surrender her body to the whim of another, overriding her basic human instincts to protect it.

The moral ties discussed above have a symbiotic relationship with the legal considerations implicated by the crime of rape. The legal system was founded by a society that felt a great deal of morality regarding crimes of sexual violence, and the foundations of the legal system were crafted to reflect and reinforce this sentiment.

Legal Considerations

A Right to the Body

John Locke was a key figure in shaping the ideals of American society. The "inalienable rights" terms by the country's forefathers were an extension of what Locke had already termed natural rights (Locke 1690: 342).

Natural rights are the undeniable rights that existed before the institution of government (ibid.). Amongst these rights, and arguably the prime example of such a right, is one's right to the body. The right to the body ensures that an individual can protect his own life and use his body as he sees fit. In this way, the right to the body allows a person to act as an autonomous individual and not a tool of society (ibid.).

Rape violates this implicit concept by overpowering the victim's discretion and protection over her body, and thus strikes as profoundly offensive.

Rape and Slavery

Consider for a moment the institution of slavery and what it meant to be a slave. Essentially, a slave was human being who was denied the property rights to his or her body. A slave was controlled by another person in order to fulfill the desires of his master.

The slave bears a striking resemblance to the rape victim in that both are so desperately lacking power that their body is forcibly controlled by the will of another. While the slave's sentence is long term, and the rape victim's is temporary, both groups experience a complete loss of control, as their bodies are used as objects intended for another's use.

The Thirteenth Amendment guarantees the right against involuntary servitude (U.S. Const. Amend. XIII). This important right does not apply solely to buying and selling slaves; it includes various forms of forced labor. Rape is comparable to involuntary servitude in that, by mere definition, it forces the victims to submit to unwanted acts in the service of another. Although slavery was the intended target of the Thirteenth Amendment, and the framers did not intend for rape to be within its scope, the two problems share a basic violation of personal autonomy which the Thirteenth Amendment aimed to eradicate.[8]

Desires versus Rights: The Extent of Desire

As evidenced, in part, by the adoption of the Thirteenth Amendment, American law places great emphasis on the value of the individual, ensuring that each individual maintains a level of autonomy. In order to accomplish this goal, one's liberty to fulfill his desires must be interrupted when it interferes with the rights of another member of society. In this way, each person maintains a range of liberty that does not impinge upon that of another; allowing all individuals to remain autonomous beings. Therefore, an attacker's desire to satisfy his own lust must be compromised when it interferes with the victim's right to her body and safety.[9]

Uncovering the Paradox

As discussed, society unwittingly perpetuates the continuation of sexual violence against women by casting them as an inferior and sexualized gender. Yet, American law preaches the fundamental ideal of the valuable individual.

While fostering an environment wrought with violence against women, the legal system seeks to maintain equal rights for all individuals. These two realities inevitably clash as society is both creating and combating sexual violence. Until this paradox is realized, the contradicting implications of social life and the legal system can not be reconciled.

Conclusion

There are many social conditions that are at play within a society where someone is sexually assaulted every two minutes and 92% of those victims are female. Beneath the conscious awareness of social relationships, women are being cast as the inferior and sexualized gender, and they are targeted for attack.

Ironically, as society perpetuates an environment ripe for sexual violence, rape carries with it a great deal of moral ties as it offends what American society, and thus American law, has adopted as core ideals and concepts. Rape victims are akin to modern day slaves as they are stripped of the right to the body and autonomy, forced to surrender their natural rights to the desires of another.

This paradoxical relationship between social norms and legal ideals is blind to the social assumptions upon which it was built, and thus society is rendered ill-equipped to end the cycle of violence against women.

Notes

1 Though women have become prevalent and effective actors in the legal field, and have made great strides in bringing about resolutions to women's issues, they are fighting their legal battles in an arena built by and for men.

2 The victims are often even given women's names.

3 The following explanations of the morally laced term "rape" are not intended to be a list of the necessary and sufficient characteristics that define the act. Instead, they are a collection of characteristics that provide some explanation for the steadfast bond between morality and rape. Other crimes, such as assault, do not encompass these characteristics, and thus they do not carry the same moral weight. It is for this reason that sexual violence and other types of physical assaults can not treated equally within the American justice system.

4 While it is true that death or suffering are both indeed choices a rape victim may have, the victim is asked to choose the least horrific option from a situation containing only the worst possible choices.

5 In many regards this belief is true, as women do lack some of the physical capabilities of males.

6 Marriage has since become far more secular in nature, and it is now regulated by the government. In that respect, the government retains a level of control over sexuality in a way that religion once did. It is for this reason that the idea of gay marriage has caused such an upheaval in the U.S. population. It does not merely challenge the government statutes, but it challenges the teachings of the religions that inspired the adoption of those statutes. I do not intend to argue for or against the legalization of gay marriage, however, it is undeniably the belief of its opposition that it can not comport with the religious aspects of traditional marriages.

7 This concept is further explained in the section titled "A Right to the Body."

8 I do not intend to argue that rape should be considered a violation of the Thirteenth Amendment. Rather, I am seeking to point out a violation of one's right to the body was considered so egregious in the context of slavery that the Thirteenth Amendment was created to eradicate it, and rape encompasses many similar violations which offend society.

9 A woman does not surrender her right to her body when she chooses to wear revealing clothing or when she becomes intoxicated. While it is true that potentially dangerous situations, such as walking alone at night, should be avoided, an attacker's desires never outweigh the victim's right to her body, and therefore it can not be said that the victim was partially at fault for the attack for failing to take such precautions.

Works Cited

Anderson, Janet et al. "Prison Rape and Sexual Coercion Behind Bars," Washington Coalition of Sexual Assault Programs 4, May, 2004, available at http://www.wcsap.org/pdf/AdEdDigestMay05.pdf.

Associated Press. 12 Boys Accused in Sexual Assault of Girl, 8, *Kansas City Channel*, May 9, 2006, available at, http://thekansascitychannel.com/news/9186245/detail.html.

Bartlett, Katherine T. "Feminist Legal Methods," 829 *Harv. L. Rev.* 103, 829–888 (1990).

Cochran, Lee. "Taboo Trial Words: 'Drunk,' 'Victim,' 'Rape,'" ABC News, Jul. 1, 2008, http://abcnews.go.com/TheLaw/story?id=5277015/.

Dictionary.com. "Rape," (last visited Jul. 22, 2008), http://dictionary.reference.com/browse/rape.

Hyams, Paul. *Marriage and Sexuality in Midevil Europe*, Cornell University, College of Arts and Sciences, 2006, http://www.arts.cornell.edu/prh3/368/index.html.

Locke, John. "A Second Treatise on Government" (1690), reprinted in *Morality and Moral Controversies*. 7, 342. Ed. John Arthur. (2005).

National Center for Victims of Crime, Sexual Assault, (last visited Jul. 22, 2008), http://www.ncvc.org/ncvc/main.aspx?dbName=DocumentViewer & DocumentID=32369.

NY PENAL §130.35.

Rape, Abuse and Incest National Network, How Often Does Sexual Assault Occur? RAINN, 2008, available at http://www.rainn.org/get-information/statistics/frequency-of-sexual-assault.

Tjaden, Patricia & Thoennes, Nancy. Full Report of the Prevalence, Incidence, and Consequences of Violence Against Women, National Institute of Justice and the Centers for Disease Control and Prevention, November, Nov., 2000, available at http://www.ncjrs.gov/txtfiles1/nij/183781.txt.

UCSC: Rape Prevention Education, Rape Statistics, (last visited Jul. 22, 2008), http://www2.ucsc.edu/rape-prevention/statistics.html/.

U.S. Const. Amend. XIII.

Westermark, Edward. "The Sources of Moral Ideas: Society, Custom and Sympathy," in *Morality and Moral Controversies* 7, 66. Ed. John Arthur. (2005).

Doniger, Wendy. "For Many Religions, Sex both Blessing and Curse," *NEWSWEEK*, Feb. 15, 2007, http://newsweek.washingtonpost.com/onfaith/wendydoniger/2007/02/sex_and_religion_joined_at_the_1.html.

Abstract

Life is a pre-requisite for justice, sustained by food and water. A justice system, too, is predicated on people being party to it. If the government as an enforcement mechanism is absent and people, who intend to self-sustain, suffer from severe dehydration and/or starvation, and they subsequently choose to violate the law, these individuals are doing the bare minimum to survive and attend trial. If these people were to act within the law's confines and stray from the legally repugnant path, they subvert their lives and the justice system's life.

A DEFENSE FOR THE LEGAL JUSTIFICATION OF NO-CHOICE SUSTENANCE CRIMES COMMITTED IN THE QUASI-HOBBESIAN STATE OF NATURE

Angela Godhwani

Introduction

As members of the animal kingdom, human beings are sustained by oxygen, food and water. This biological trinity of necessities propels organ-function and the bodily processes requisite for life. People have needs because their lives are dependent on the aforementioned forms of sustenance. Unlike lower sentient beings, which also have needs, humans are born with the capacity to rationalize. A rational man is capable of making choices and can engage in plans of action. Laws are implemented in our world to prevent the deleterious actions that would otherwise fester in an unregulated natural state; conjunctionally, they serve to protect citizens from crime.

Hobbes' theory of a war of all, against all, becomes reality when men are unwillingly isolated from their sovereigns. Survival becomes the individual's prerogative alone because no sovereign exists to accept her burden. Unlike a Hobbesian state of nature, which has no installed legal enforcement mechanism, in a "quasi-Hobbesian state of nature," civilization's laws are temporarily suspended because the sovereign's presence is unwillingly absent. Denizens pre-exposed to the rules of a sovereign thusly populate the quasi-Hobbesian state, but these rules are going un-enforced.

Under such dire circumstances, a hybrid of natural law and civilization's laws govern rational people's consciences. Vigilantism abounds because (the below are not empirical claims, but their consequences will be explored if this premise is granted):

1. Men feel insecure because they are vulnerable in the absence of their government.
2. Men internalize this fear and act to preserve and protect themselves because no one else will.

In this paper, I will argue that individuals in these "no-choice" positions ought to be legally justified (provided they are not already so) in performing sustenance-related crimes, if their *intent* is to access nourishment and hydration. I will proceed to argue this claim under the following premises:

1. Morals exist in the quasi-Hobbesian state of nature. Breaching one's morals entails rational forethought; such acts are thus deliberated acts of conscientious refusal.
2. Nature coerces men to fuel themselves with food and water. Choosing to perpetually starve and be dehydrated defies the coercive nature of nature.
3. If an individual's intentions are not to preserve her endangered life and fulfill her primary needs, the law is then justified in punishing her.

The state of the Asian nations affected in the aftermath of the 2004 Sumatra-Andaman earthquake and its tsunami, as well as the moral climate aboard the *Mignonette* in *Regina v. Dudley and Stephens* provide conditions of two diametrically opposed no-choice situations and quasi-Hobbesian states of nature. From this frame, I will argue that grave acts of desperation should be allotted for, if they are committed to sustain their performers' lives.

The No-Choice Situation

A Hypothetical Example

A student is running unopposed for president in his class elections. If everyone votes against him and no alternative candidates are elected, his classmates' sentiments will not be accurately reflected. Given that 1) choice exists because of freedom and 2) choice is the freedom to decide between plural ends (multiple alternatives), if there is only one end available, by definition, a choice cannot be made. If only one option exists, it is entered into by default; therefore, this does not reflect the chooser's will.

Likewise, when an individual stands between the choices of death and committing a morally repugnant deed, his freedom of choice is extinguished. Choosing death theoretically constitutes a choice. Choosing not to choose is also sought in death, but in a true no-choice situation, only one alternative is available. Life is the singular alternative because choosing death ultimately terminates choice and the potential to make future choices. Death eradicates choice because in this state, a person is no longer a person, just as a slave is no longer a person (but property). Unless we or some other individual takes away our life, nature will intervene and death will occur on its own. We have no choice to be born, and we have no choice to die.

Guidelines to Test Whether or Not a Situation May Be Classified as "No-Choice"

1. Death, or committing some legally reprehensible deed to prevent death is the only foreseeable option.
2. Individuals divided between life and death are coerced into this position.

We Don't Make the Cut

Euthanasia, suicide, and abortion do not constitute no-choice situations because each generates multiple options. A palliative-care patient can choose to take morphine for his pain, rather than resort to physician-assisted suicide. A woman contemplating abortion can carry her fetus to term and put her child up for adoption. Likewise, a person contemplating suicide can undergo therapy. No-choice situations differ from the above because morphine, therapy, and abortion/adoption constitute alternatives to life and death.

When a person's only choices are life and death and she "chooses" death, she is both:

1. Coerced.[1]
2. Choosing to stop choosing for the rest of her life.

Examples Where Death Appears to be a Choice

One can argue that a Japanese warrior who sacrifices his life for honor is making a valid choice. The warrior, however, is choosing between cowardice and honor, not life and death. He is not in a no-choice situation and can continue to live dishonorably.

An imprudent farmer who squandered his time, fails to store enough food for the winter, and then chooses to rob his neighbor's foodstuffs is not trapped in a no-choice situation. This foolish farmer chose to "dig his own grave." A no-choice situation features a definitive coercive mechanism, which excises the individual's will from a situation. If the farmer planted his crops earlier, he could have easily prevented his misery and ensured himself a sizeable food-supply. He had a choice and its consequences were reasonably expectable.

Unlike a lazy farmer, the victim of an earthquake cannot anticipate when a natural disaster will occur (with the exception of earth scientists, seismologists, etc.); but, he can ensure that his home is sturdy going forward (particularly if the individual's geographic location has been historically notorious for earthquakes). Concurrently, ships are equipped with lifeboats, life vests, and food supplies. The chances of being adrift at sea are highly probable during inclement weather; though oftentimes, necessary precautions are inadequate. People will continue to be caught off-guard because meteorology is imperfect and it was even further from perfection in the past.

Sustenance as Bondate, Sustenance as an Absolute Right

If self-preservation through nourishment were not an absolute right (meaning that it is an unconditional and unquestionable need) then water fountains would not be found in public libraries or governmental offices, and jails would not provide criminals with meals. Primary needs are requirements. The perpetual deprivation of these sustaining "ingredients" ultimately yields death. Unlike plants, people cannot perform photosynthesis and thrive off sunlight and/or the occasional downpour. Hunger and thirst are egalitarian, fettering infants and kings alike without their consent. To ensure the proper functioning of their bodily processes, and thus their lives, people require externally acquired energy. People do not choose to be endowed with life, nor to be enslaved by the primary needs upon which their lives depend. They are simply born, and accordingly, coerced by their bodies and its needs.

Hobbe's State of Nature, Distilled

To further comprehend the "quasi-Hobbesian state of nature," it is first essential to understand the parameters of the Hobbesian state of nature. According to Hobbes, a war of all against all is inevitable when men are ungoverned by a sovereign. Dismal about human nature, Hobbes believes that amongst men, peace is only attainable under an overarching state. A sovereign-free anarchical state is constantly reigned by warfare.[2] Men, in the "state of nature" are equal in body and mind, and they are equally vulnerable. Rational men have the capacity to deliberate and to take effective means to their ends to survive. Imprudent, irrational men hinder themselves from overcoming their obstacles. Neither justice nor injustice exist in this state; they are characteristics of civilization.

In the natural world, ownership and safety are ephemeral; a man's life is "solitary, poor, nasty, brutish, and short," according to Hobbes. His survival is subject to himself alone. People have the same need to survive and competition creates a frenzied state of diffidence. Alliances can be sought in the Hobbesian state, reflecting man's social nature, but eventually his allies will become his foes when they compete for the same resources. These alliances will break because the state of nature's fundamental right is self-preservation achieved by following the three fundamental laws of nature:

- Rule 1—Seek peace if it is obtainable. If peace is unattainable, one's ends may be sought through war.
- Rule 2—People should give up their rights to pursue things if others agree to give up rights/interests as well.
- Rule 3—You must do what the sovereign orders.[3]

If this chaotic state of nature reigned, men would kill for the resources they wanted and the whole world would eventually be annihilated.

A Quasi-Hobbesian State of Nature

Civilized societies populated by socially interdependent beings are governed by the laws of markets, and by the laws of the justice system. Unlike an absolute state of nature where chaos is law, in a "quasi-Hobbesian state of nature," the morals and laws of the civilized world exist. People in a quasi-Hobbesian state of nature are protected by the construct of societal laws, but in their circumstances, abiding by these laws will result in their deaths. If they survive, they will face civilized societies' justice system.[4] It is argued that society is like a leviathan because it enforces its own social moral code through criticism and guilt, without formal punishment of law. Individuals in the quasi-Hobbesian state of nature are a microcosm of society, and the societal construct of morals and laws (barring amnesia) remain. Residents have to balance their innate instincts for survival with the legal standards internalized from life in the civilized world. If a governmental enforcement mechanism is unwillingly absent, people have to rely on themselves to survive.

Constructs of rights exists in this state, but once again, no authoritarian figures are available to protect and adjudicate. Resultantly, civilization's rights are rendered obsolete and natural rights are installed in their absence, by default.

The Crux of it All

Choosing to break the law after careful deliberation, rather than on impulse, may be classified as an act of conscientious refusal. If conscientious refusal of the law is the only means of attaining nourishment in severe malnutrition and dehydration's glare, this act is justified, provided that the refuser's sole intent is to survive, and no law enforcers are present to help.[5]

The theoretical Hobbesian state of nature is different from the legal and moral climate *Regina v. Dudley and Stephens* besets, and from the 2004 Asian tsunami, whose destructive trail spawned theft-crimes to feed primary needs. Though the victims of each scenario were isolated from their sovereigns, some semblance of government and justice remained. In vulnerable states of isolation, when trapped in a no-choice situation, people are endowed with the natural instinct to survive; though laws may prohibit their survival, if they do not survive, I argue that law has failed in its purpose to protect people from chaos.

Regina v. Dudley and Stephens, Examined

One thousand six hundred miles from the Cape of Good Hope, four men, Dudley, Stephens, Parker, and Brooks took to a lifeboat from their yacht, after being cast away by a storm on July 5, 1884. The lifeboat's only contents were two one-pound tins of turnips. Three days after consuming these, the men were left hungry. On day four, save for rainwater caught in oilskin capes, a small turtle was their only form of sustenance. On the eighteenth day, perhaps 1000 miles from land, without food in their systems for seven days and without water for five, if no relief arrived, the men spoke of sacrificing Parker, their crew-member. Brooks refused the proposition and Parker was not consulted. On July 24th Dudley re-suggested they choose a sacrifice from amongst the lot, so the rest could be saved. Brooks dissented again. Parker, who was without family, was chosen as the sacrifice without his consent. The following morning, Dudley proposed murdering Parker, provided that no vessel was in sight. Stephens agreed with Dudley the next fruitless morning. Brooks dissented again and was told to nap. On this day, Dudley killed a feeble, famine-ravished Parker and "... offered a prayer asking forgiveness for them all if either of them should be tempted to commit a rash act, and that their souls might be saved" ("Survival on a Lifeboat" 277). All three men (Brooks the dissenter included) fed on Parker's carcass and blood for four days. On the fourth day, a vessel rescued the three men. Within the four days, between Parker's murder and the rescue, it was determined that famine would have murdered the men and the weakened Parker would have died either way.

The legal question subsequently posed is whether two family-men, adrift at sea for a period of twenty days, facing certain death, were legally justified in murdering a dying seventeen- or eighteen-year-old boy for their own personal sustenance. The major argument of Sir H. James for the Crown and the prosecution was that Parker was not harming the other men in any way. The murder did not constitute self-defense, the only legal means of taking a life. Additionally, the act did not prevent Parker from gravely harming some third party ("Survival on a Lifeboat" 278). The defense argued that self-preservation and necessity are within the parameters of a justification.[6] The judges concluded that murder is only justified when committed in self-defense; Dudley and Stephens' act of murdering Parker to sustain their own lives was an act of temptation, not necessity. The two men were ultimately convicted with murder. Eventually, the Queen lowered the severity of their sentences, but the murder remained one of first-degree. Brooks, the fourth person involved, did not intend to kill Parker, nor did he agree to his murder. Brooks was not guilty of murder, but he was guilty of benefiting from the crime ("Survival on a Lifeboat" 281–286).

Stephens and Dudley knew that they were committing an egregiously violent act because they offered a prayer admitting so. If national rescue parties could save every man adrift at sea, then these men would be unjustified in their actions. Since this is infeasible and these men were stranded, coerced by time, famine and dehydration, their circumstances must be taken into account. The party was directly subjected to the laws of nature, and if they survived, to the laws of civilization. Their morally and legally reprehensible decisions were wrong from the civilized world's perspective, but their dilemma took place in another one.[7]

At trial, Judge Coleridge declares that temptation is not an excuse. It is easy for him to state that morality and law are separate entities, and then proclaim: "[t]o preserve one's life is generally speaking a duty, but it may be the plainest and highest duty to sacrifice it. War is full of instances in which it is a man's duty not to live, but to die . . ." ("Survival on a Lifeboat" 280). Self-sacrifice for valor and glory in war are applauded because these deaths serve a nation and a purpose. Brooks dissented from murdering Parker and though moral in this decision, he did eat the flesh and blood of the boy. Brook's primary needs were unfulfilled and therefore his crime, as well as Dudley and Stephens', ought to be classified as necessities. Temptations are dispensable wants and desires. In short, life will continue without them. A man cannot be tempted to inhale air; without it, he would suffocate and die. He **needs** it.

According to Coleridge, fulfilling one's primary needs in the name of self-defense is impermissible. After all, Parker, the murdered boy, had his own unfulfilled primary needs and he was harming no one. The men on-ship tried to "seek peace" by biding their time, and by prolonging their suffering in their internal and external battle against nature. However, self-defense denotes protecting oneself from harm. Could I stand in Dudley or Stephen's shoes, I would infer that my crime was neither one of temptation nor one of self-defense. I would label it a "sustenance-related" crime, juxtaposed against a no-choice situation backdrop. If you recall, the no-choice provisions include: 1) Death, or committing some legally reprehensible deed to prevent death are the only foreseeable options; 2) Individuals divided between life and death are coerced into this position. The men, in this case, were coerced by their bodies and by nature; thus, they did what they could to sustain themselves.

The men aboard the lifeboat could have taken intermediary steps to fulfill their primary needs. For instance, they could have consumed one limb of Parker's at a time, until their next incremental "feeding." Parker may not have died if part of his leg was amputated, but a painful life would be inevitable in this anesthesia-devoid time period.

The desperate measures taken in this case are morally and legally wrong under the contemporary American justice system, as well as through the lens of 19th-century England's justice system. According to Judge Brandt's definition of a justification, Dudley and Stephens did not act in reasonable self-defense. Parker did not threaten the men and if they failed to act, Parker was not harming them. However, if these individuals were not subject to external coercion from nature and internal coercion from their starving bodies, divided between life and death, there would have been no need to deliberately murder Parker.

Brandt's third provision, defining a legal justification states that: "[o]ne may perform a forbidden act with impunity if, in case one does not, the result one causes and worse will in all probability happen anyway. For instance, one judge has indicated that a seaman is not liable for putting persons out of an over-crowded lifeboat in a storm, if otherwise, the boat would sink, provided the selection of the unfortunates is made in a reasonable manner" (283). Barring their rescue, if Dudley and Stephens did not murder Parker, all four men would inevitably have perished. In the utilitarian sense, the men were justified in taking Parker's life by saving the greatest number of people feasible under their circumstances. This paper, however, is not structured to be a utilitarian argument.

I believe the unspoken sentiments and connotations derived from the practice of cannibalism were reduced to a standard label of murder. Cannibalism was being tried because most murderers do not have to consume their victim's flesh to survive. Judge Coleridge pronounces that such trials are difficult to judge because the judge may be unable to live up to the standards he adjudicates, nor abide by conventions, which he cannot necessarily fulfill ("Survival on a Lifeboat" 280). Accordingly, this gives rise to the conundrum of proceeding by a constitution forged by cannibals that governs men and prescribes the best hands to do its biddings. The criteria that appointed Judge Coleridge the best man for his job would consequently make him the worst. If Coleridge represents the will of his society, he also admits that he may be unable to satisfy the standards even he sets. Should authoritarians be as fallible as the people they govern, the system that distinguishes famine from temptation is inherently flawed. If even the "cultured" English can succumb to cannibalism, then these savage instincts are latent within each of us. If this were not true, Queen Regina would not have reduced Dudley and Stephen's death sentence to six months of imprisonment. The men would have unjustly died under laws that could neither fluctuate nor realistically gauge their circumstances. When law's interpreters are uncertain of whether or not they would comply with it, the law's value is undermined. The government has a right to punish its citizens where it sees fit, but it should do so when it can hold itself up to the same standards.

Excluded from Coleridge's judgment was a suggestion made by his brother, Grove. Grove suggested that if Stephens and Dudley were initially justified in killing Parker, then if two of the three remaining men murdered another crewman to save themselves, and one of the two men remaining did the same, only one individual would survive. As Coleridge stated, the time of the men's rescue was arbitrary. It is possible that the men on board could have been rescued seconds before slashing Parker's throat, but this did not happen. Also, a rescue vessel could have discovered them after killing Parker, before they even consumed his flesh. Since their entire purpose in murdering Parker was to consume his flesh to save themselves, their intent remains constant. They waited until they could wait no more. Stephens and Dudley thus chose the only option that provided options.

Tragedy is when three men are rescued, though all four have the right to live. A man's right to his body, his self-ownership, is violated if he is murdered (Boaz 64). Parker did not use his right to survive because he was unable to. He was weak and dying and if in Hobbes' state of nature, he would have been killed. In the quasi-Hobbesian realm under which his murder took place, the committed act was deliberated under a semblance of existing morals and laws. What-ifs and perhaps are taken into account when a man is rationally deliberating. Dudley and Stephens recognized the weight of their actions because they come from a moral society and still chose what they did to save themselves.

Foreseeability

Meteorology in 1884, without the aid of technology, was glaringly more primitive than it is today. Being adrift at sea was foreseeable, but not to the extent that it currently is. Prior to taking Parker's life, Dudley and Stephens "offered" a prayer with full knowledge that murdering Parker was unacceptable. This displays remorse and forethought. Parker was not murdered in vain, but with reason. The men chose not to abide by the laws of England, but in doing so, they survived and therefore chose life (the only option that allows for choice to exist). Rather than promoting eating your crewmates, this case deters similar future acts from occurring. It provides a cautionary tale for sailors to adequately supply their vessels and to refrain from traveling in brutal weather. Unlike the foolish farmer that had a greater degree of foreseeability (but chose to steal his neighbors crops rather than plant his own) the men in this case, did not. If one does not plant seeds, one will not have crops.[8] If one goes outside without an umbrella on a sunny day, he may return home drenched, but this is less foreseeable.

Foreseeability also plays a major role in highlighting which morally repugnant acts are, and are not justified in no-choice situations. Victims of the 2005 Hurricane Katrina who chose not to abide by severe weather storm warnings for instance, live in the Gulf Coast area which is notorious for hurricanes striking. Not evacuating is imprudent and if people knew the gravity of their situations beforehand and still refused to listen, then the fault is theirs alone. Though it may be treacherously icy on the roads, ambulances still have to run, and people will continue to go to work, taking a risk, rather than guaranteeing a lost paycheck. There is a certain element of risk in every endeavor, if there were not, dangerous, but high paying professions would become more populated. When we board a plane or drive a vehicle, this can be our final journey though we may not actively anticipate this. The parameters of foreseeability will fluctuate from case to case; but, the justice system can use foreseeability as a yardstick. Most often, chaotic scenarios such as no-choice situations are beyond the scope of measurement. Tragedy, after all, is immeasurable and is relative to the person experiencing it. But, I believe the degree of forseeability and the crime (if one must be charged) ought to be directly correlated, if the justice system chooses to gauge tragedy.

Natural Disaster and Quasi-Natural Law

The 2004 Asian tsunami, a result of an earthquake, left citizens of Indonesia, Sri Lanka, South India, and Thailand in subhuman conditions. Its devastation was felt even in the distant nations of Bangladesh, India, Malaysia,

Myanmar, Thailand, Singapore and the Maldives. Disaster relief was scarce if provided, and a general state of chaos reigned because of multiplying water borne diseases and the lack of food and clean water.[9] The tsunami left the framework of a quasi-Hobbesian state of nature in its wake. Without humanitarian aid to satisfy people's unfulfilled primary needs, many were left without an incentive to abide by the law. In fact, law enforcers such as policemen are equally stranded and are thus equally as helpless as the citizens they protect.

Conscientious Refusal

If there are no other alternatives available to residents, meaning they transfixed between life and death alone and they conscientiously refuse to obey the law, then they are justified in looting. Conscientious refusal "... is noncompliance with a more or less direct legal injunction or administrative order. It is refusal since an order is addressed to us, and given the nature of the situation, whether we accede to it is known to the authorities" (Rawls 369). Conscientious refusal *may* be grounded on political principles whereas civil disobedience *is* grounded on them. The conscientious refuser, unlike the civil disobedient is not a minority seeking change in the majority/public forum, or the brand of justice in place, but rather he is openly refusing to obey a law or a direct legal order. Unlike his disobedient counterpart, the refuser is not appealing to the majority's sense of justice; he is more pessimistic than a civil disobedient because he "... may entertain no expectation of changing laws or policies" (Rawls 369).

In the quasi-Hobbesian scenario constructed in the wake of this tsunami, no-choice sustenance related crimes are not performed in vain: "[t]hose ready to withhold obedience recognize that there may be no basis for mutual understanding; they do not seek out occasions for disobedience as a way to state their cause. *Rather, they bide their time hoping that the necessity to disobey will not arise* ... they may entertain no expectation of changing laws or policies" (ibid.). In my examples, the crimes committed are contingent on the intention to acquire sustenance, with the actor's possession of their full rational faculties, knowing that they may be penalized for doing so.

Measuring "Dire"

A no-choice sustenance related crime ought to be legally justified in the civilized world, provided that the circumstances are dire. If "no-choice," as I define it, entails an individual standing between some coercive force or death, it may be argued that for each moment they live, they are also dying. A person who hates his life, for example, may view it as a coercive force. This person may also view severe starvation as being a few french fries short of a Happy Meal™. Though what constitutes a "dire circumstance" is relative from case to case, I will attempt to provide a yardstick for consistency's sake.

An individual can survive for approximately four days without water and thirty to forty days without food. If I am the victim of a titanic tsunami, per se, and I go without water for two days, my need for water is great, but it is not yet detrimental. I am still halfway to being "dire" if I can go for four without. As a general rule then, if an individual is beyond three-quarters on the road to being "dire" or in grave danger (time-wise), then, I argue that their conditions are severe. Theoretically, from an outsiders' stance it is easy to state that two is halfway to four and that three is three-quarters, or that twenty-five days without food is dire and fifteen is not. If I am actually facing starvation and dehydration, the combination of the two can have mortal implications in a shorter period than when faced individually. In suit, I cannot formulaically pinpoint when I am closer to death but can feel pain, and my tolerance-level should be at the brink of exhaustion. What is the brink of exhaustion? I will state three days without water and twenty-five days without food constitute "dire," if suffered individually. When in combination, "dire" will be two days without water and fifteen without food, the halfway-point for each. Skeptics can easily question why "dire" isn't a minute under three days, or a second over twenty-five. If there is no set bracket, then an individual who misses one meal may claim that they are severely malnourished and on the brink of death. Scientists may have a different measuring system, and because I am a student of philosophy, I will adhere to my guidelines and leave the science to the scientists.

Our need for food and water is constant. People naturally require a greater amount of water than food because dehydration kills before starvation does. A man is therefore entitled to steal water for four days because he will die without it in this span of time. He is entitled to steal a day's worth of food until he needs to steal again, because food has less sustaining power than water. Stealing beyond this amount places greed before immediate need. Only theft of the bare minimum should be lawful, so that an individual can survive to face trial.

Explanatory Hypothetical Situations

If I suffer from a medical condition, which requires the constant hydration of my body, then my need is greater than the average man's. I am justified in stealing water if my physician pre-informs me of my condition and there are no other legal or moral means to obtain the water.

In a no-choice situation, a man is not justified in stealing enough food to last him a year. Though men need a constant supply of food, no-choice situations span a month long, a time-period under which an individual can survive without food.

If an entire yacht hit an iceberg in the year 2006 and its occupants were stranded at sea, relief would come more speedily than in the 1800s due to scientific and technological advancements.

Conditions Ripen for Governmental Neglect

Due to the rare nature of the presented cases, the government can down-play its accountability because: a once-in-a-century event has the same likelihood of occurring at the beginning or end of a century. Second, risks are ignored because taking precautions demands officials within a centralized government "... to respond to the full spectrum of possible risks against which cost-justified measures might be taken." Government officials can simply attend to a variety of other matters before focusing their attention on less pressing ones. Third, wealthy nations may perceive that they are "free-rided" upon by their less wealthy counterparts. Concurrently, the wealthy nations may feel less apt to assist financially if they do not expect reciprocity in some form. Fourth, impoverished nations are unable to take cost-justified precautions because their governments are either "weak, inefficient, or corrupt." It will be difficult for them to act as a legal enforcement mechanism in times of crisis.

Fifth, there is a lack of political support for financing low-probability disasters that people ignore, because people do not usually think in terms of probability (Posner).

The Asian tsunami was a low-probability/ high-cost risk, which the Pacific nations refused to invest precautionary measures into, by extending their pre-existing tsunami warning system to the Indian Ocean before the natural disaster occurred. Slight risks are ignored for political reasons and therein resides the problem. This creates a niche for governmental neglect.

Storeowners and Price Gougers

Economies and markets, just like the justice system, would cease to exist if there were no participants within or under them. In the quasi-Hobbesian state, a store-owner requires sustenance, as does the robber who steals from him. Though the store-owner's livelihood is threatened when he is robbed, the individual's right to life trumps the store-owner's economic losses in a state of emergency. The store-owner can justifiably harm the robber to keep his own primary sources of sustenance, if his circumstances are dire. Though he may suffer the consequences of his actions when the state of emergency becomes a state of normalcy, he cannot retroactively change what he has done. He would not be alive to engage in future market transactions if he had not chosen to violate the law to save his life.

It is true that a storeowner has the right to profit from the sale of his goods, because in Locke's view, he has put his labor into this task and would otherwise have no financial incentive to sell. This is his trade and his means of sustaining himself. If a storeowner chooses to price-gouge, this is arbitrary in the quasi-Hobbesian state. I do not advocate price-gouging, nor being Robin Hood or Raskolnikov and stealing from the rich to help the poor. My focus is strictly on dire circumstances and ends.

Hoarding, Luxuries, and the Chivalrous Man

In a quasi-Hobbesian state of nature, crimes committed with intentions straying from the basic preservation of life, ought not be legally justified in the civilized world. A person should be penalized by the civilized world's justice system for acts performed where her primary need fulfillment does not comport with her intent. A woman, for example, who steals a Prada bag because she believes she will die without it, should not be legally justified by the civilized world's standards. The pre-requisite for the justice system is life. A Prada bag is a luxury. Though the justice system cannot live without people, people can live without luxuries. If filet mignon, normally considered a luxury meal is the only food available to a starving man, under the scenario and guidelines I have created, he is justified in attaining it. If he steals filet mignon instead of hamburger meat to survive, both are forms of sustenance and justifiable, but greed or a more refined palate are linked to this crime.

If a man chooses to steal an amount of water beyond what is necessary to sustain him, and he hordes it while others die around him, he is unjustified in taking too much. Though he ought to help his neighbors and share the water he has stolen, he is not obligated to do so. This individual did not create the parched throats of his neighbors, their own bodies did. Chivalrous men, who kill or steal, to help people who cannot help themselves, may be noble in their actions, but this may not comply legally. The chivalrous utilitarian can take the risk to help others, but it is up to civilized society's justice system to decide his outcome.

The Fetus in the Quasi-Hobbesian State

A man does not have to steal food for his wife; his life is not dependent on hers. He existed before he married her, and therefore he can exist without her, and vice versa. However, a man is obligated to help his pregnant wife because he helped create the fetus, which has its own primary needs. A fetus is incapable of defending itself, and since it is implanted in a woman's body, she too is justified in committing no-choice crimes to sustain it. The fetus would not exist if its creators did not first exist. The same ideally goes for obligations to children who are equally solely dependent on their parents, until they are capable of sustaining themselves.

The Government

The Federal Emergency Management Agency (FEMA), the U.S. Coast Guard, the Army, the Navy and police officers exist to help when natural or other disasters strike in America. If these groups are unavailable to perform their function in society, then people who choose the criminal junction for primary sustenance are justified in assuming their position, if there is absolutely no other means of legally doing so. It is within the government's jurisdiction to decide the point if, and at which it failed to do its job, and where the choices of the criminal's "undertaking" of the government's job ends. If it does not take into account its own inadequacies and punishes no-choice nourishment victims to the fullest extent of the law, it is wrong in doing so. Fulfilling one's primary needs are the bare minimum required for survival, and if people are not legally allowed to survive, then government is indirectly promoting death. It would then be failing to promote people's positive and negative liberties. In the cases described, death was inevitable and choices did not exist, so the law should take this into account and should not penalize these acts. If the law fails to see an individual's actions as being justified, it has the right to penalize this person. There are disparities between what the conscientious refuser sees as justified, and what the law views it to be and so punishment will continue to occur. This is the way, and reason why government works. However, if the conditions which I have outlined frame a crime and are the reason for its existence, then the government is not justified in penalizing these refusers.

Anything Does Not Go

This principle is not a garden variety "anything goes" matter. If people steal cigarettes or alcohol, which they argue they are dependent on, in the quasi-Hobbesian state of nature, they are unjustified because other individuals abstain from consuming/smoking them and still survive. The chain smoker or alcoholic's quality of life may deteriorate, but their lives will not. Any other exceptions would no longer entail questions of need, but questions of want. If an asthmatic steals Albuterol, since her life is dependent on it, she is justified in attaining it. The same goes for other life-sustaining medications.

Intent and the Doctrine of Double Effect

In the quasi-Hobbesian state, stealing a plasma screen television, per se, ought to be legally justified if a starving robber's direct intent is limited to exchanging it for comestibles. Acquinas' doctrine of double effect states that an act which harms is a side effect of another act which promotes something good. It is similar to an act, done in the name of the "greater good," for instance, landing a plane with twenty passengers into a nearby ocean to prevent an entire village from being murdered. The side effect is death, but it has also ensured the safety of the village. So a television stolen, though not legally or morally correct, is more permissible and does not compare to the good of preventing unnecessary physical human pain and suffering which is far more intense than the loss of a television.[10]

Rape in the Quasi-Hobbesian State

If rape is committed in the quasi-Hobbesian state of nature, it is unjustified because it preserves the quality of a deviant's life, not the life itself. Reproduction is a byproduct of rape, but reproduction is not necessary to sustain an individual's life, though it may sustain future populations. Life gives an individual the ownership of their body, unless they are a slave. A fetus, if not intentionally desired to occupy one's body, violates an individual's right to the ownership of their body. Reproduction is a biological necessity ensuring the survival of mankind, but rape is a biological temptation that can be suppressed and/or ignored.

In a prison setting where rape is a means of stratifying the tough guys from the weaklings, and often a means of survival, rape is still unjustified because it violates the ownership of the victim's body. If a starving individual has to choose between being raped in exchange for food, or continuing to starve, this does not constitute a no-choice situation. Rape cannot be chosen because by nature, this crime is committed without the consent of its victim.

Kleptomaniacs

A kleptomaniac, who cannot "survive" without their supposed wants, will definitely die without food and water. The individual's compulsive behavior muddies the distinction between conscientiously refusing the law to survive and simply furthering his own ends. A dying kleptomaniac is justified in pillaging for primary sustenance if it will prevent his death. If the kleptomaniac is not dying, his fate and the accountability of his actions are in the hands of the justice system.

Acts of God

Government and disaster relief organizations such as FEMA exist to combat acts of God. These acts blaze trails of chaos, are not manmade and require active effort to jumpstart normalcy's return. The government's capacity to prevent disaster is limited. This is evident through the existence of private medical care, private life/auto/flood insurance and private pharmaceutical companies. If there were enough privatized disaster relief organizations to ameliorate stricken areas and peoples, the government could permissibly step aside and direct their attentions elsewhere. The government, however, would be responsible for ensuring the relief agencies' lawfulness. Unless disaster relief programs are infinitely efficient and can ensure coverage for all victims, government intervention is necessary. Governmental neglect to detect future potential disasters would be unjustified and would engender vigilantism. However, an absolute state of preparedness is unrealistic; the government is naturally flawed. Therefore, the government ought to factor this into its decision-making process before punishing act of God "vigilantes."

Conclusion

The men aboard the *Marionette* did not choose to be adrift at sea, out of the reach of civilization, and in the throes of extreme dehydration and famine. Stephens and Dudley succumbed to murder and cannibalism to survive in the *Regina v. Dudley and Stephens* case. They chose not to die in the name of valor or God, as merited by the judge presiding over their trial. Dudley and Stephens chose to live. Men who choose to sustain their own lives by taking other's are often labeled cowards; the men, in this case, chose the only alternative available to them. They bided their time as conscientious refusers and acted when they could no longer wait. In the post-Enlightenment world of England, where primitive practices were taboo, this case lives on as a paradigm of civilized man's susceptibility to death.

Likewise, in the wake of the 2004 Asian tsunami, the force of law disintegrates when the law enforcers are in the same dire straits as the people they supervise. When victims of major natural disasters do not have access to basic necessities such as water and food, faith in their government will logically erode, and its flaws will be exposed. Citizens in no-choice situations are justified in pursuing life because the government is not available to assist them, and often, not available to assist itself.

The seemingly unlawful acts of rational pillagers, murderers and cannibals become justified when and if they are under the umbrella of a quasi-Hobbesian state, in a no-choice situation. Victims in both scenarios are pre-exposed to society's laws and will be re-exposed to its justice system if they survive. Doing anything beyond the bare minimum to sustain oneself from the internal and external coercive forces of nature may not be defensible in the justice system's eyes and should be deemed criminal in nature. If the victims' conduct is contextually within reason, by refusing the law, this person is respecting the law by staying alive to attend trial.

Aside from a masochist, a philosopher, or someone suicidal, the epicenter of a no-choice situation is not the rational, prudent man's vacation spot. To ensure an equitable legal system, laws that govern life ought to cater to the uncertainty that defines it. Situational permutations must be taken into account while consistency should be delicately balanced. Unfortunate victims will continue to be immersed in cross-fire situations. For those who will, a justice system that can expand and accommodate the unlikely, factoring its own imperfections can help to relinquish them.

Notes

1 I define coercion as the undue influence on an individual's ability to freely choose. Whether it be physical, non-physical, internal, external, explicit, implicit, and/or in the form of a threat, every manifestation of coercion unduly subverts a person's will.

2 "Where there is no common power, there is no law; where no law, no injustice. Force and fraud are in war the two cardinal virtues. Justice and injustice are none of the faculties neither of the body nor mind. If they were, they might be in a man that were alone in the world, as well as his senses and passions. They are qualities that relate to men in society, not in solitude. It is consequent also to the same condition that there is no propriety, no dominion, no mine and thine distinct; but only that to be every man's that he can get, and for so long as he can keep it. And thus much for the ill condition which man by mere nature is actually placed in, though with a possibility to come out of it consisting partly in the passions, partly in his reason" (Hobbes 108).

3 Special thanks to Professor John Arthur for distilling and clarifying these rules.

4 An exception to this claim would involve groups considered their own nations, such as Native Americans who have their own sovereigns, but even they will face the American justice system if they act beyond the guidelines covered in their own laws.

5 A recluse who chooses to geographically divorce herself from society does not qualify as a denizen of my theoretical state. If she were trapped against her will without anyone to assist her escape, the coercive nature of the situation would then qualify. If this woman was rescued and was discovered to have acted unlawfully, she would still be subject to the justice system when re-immersed in the civilized world.

6 Self-preservation, as I define it, is when a man chooses his own life where the life of another will inevitably depart. Necessity as I define it, is an act which would otherwise be a crime, but the circumstances it is committed under negate its criminal classification.

7 Though what is right and wrong in the civilized world is arguable, cannibalism remains a societal taboo and first-degree murderers are still tried in courts of law.

8 One can have crops if they do not plant them via trade, bartering, etc. but they will not be the very plants which they grew, themselves.

9 This information was discerned from graphic news broadcasts at the time.

10 Special thanks to Steven Scalet, Ph.D. for bringing this doctrine to my attention.

Works Cited

Aquinas, Thomas. (1988). (13th c). *Summa Theologica II-II*, Q. 64, art. 7, "Of Killing," in *On Law, Morality, and Politics.* Indianapolis/Cambridge: Hackett Publishing Co. Eds. William P. Baumgarth and Richard J. Regan, S. J. pp. 226–227.

Berlin, I. (1970). "Two Concepts of Liberty," in I. Berlin, *Four Essays on Liberty.* New York: Oxford University Press, pp. 118–172.

Boaz, David. (1997). *Libertarianism: A Primer*. New York: The Free Press.

Brandt, Richard B. (1959). "The Principles of Criminal Law." In J. Arthur and W. H. Shaw (3rd ed.) *Readings in the Philosophy of Law.* Upper Saddle River, NJ: Prentice Hall, pp. 281–286.

Hobbes, Thomas. (1958). *Leviathan Parts I and II.* New York: The Liberal Arts Press, Inc.

Hume, David. (1978). "Justice and Property," from *A Treatise of Human Nature,* 2nd ed. Ed. L. A. Selby-Bigge. Oxford: Clarendon, pp. 484–88, 494–98, 514, 526. In *The Libertarian Reader: Classic & Contemporary Writings from Lao-Tzu to Milton Friedman.* Ed. David Boaz. New York: The Free Press, 1997, pp. 135–139.

Kant, Immanuel. (1991). "Equality of Rights," from *Kant: Political Writings,* Ed. Hans Reiss, trans. H. B. Nisbet, Cambridge: Cambridge University Press, pp. 73–85, 137. In *The Libertarian Reader: Classic & Contemporary Writings from Lao-Tzu to Milton Friedman.* Ed. David Boaz. New York: The Free Press, 1997, pp. 142–148.

Kant, Immanuel. (1963). *Lecture on Ethics.* Trans. Louis Infield. Gloucester: Harper & Row.

Kipnis, Kenneth. (1976). "*Criminal Justice and the Negotiated Plea.*" In J. Arthur and W. H. Shaw (3rd ed.) *Readings in the Philosophy of Law.* Upper Saddle River, NJ: Prentice Hall, pp. 378–385.

Posner, Richard. (2006). "The Tsunami and the Economics of Catastrophic Risk." [Weblog entry.] The Becker-Posner Blog. 5 Jan 2005. http://www.becker-posner-blog.com/archives/2005/01/the_tsunami_and.html. 16 Feb 2006.

Rand, Ayn. (1961). "The Objectivist Ethics," from a talk given at the University of Wisconsin in 1961 in *The Ayn Rand Reader.* Eds. Gary Hull and Leonard Peikoff, pp. 84–93.

Rawls, John. (1971). *A Theory of Justice*. Cambridge: The Belknap Press of Harvard University Press.

"Survival on a Lifeboat: *The Queen v. Dudley and Stephens.*" From *Law Reports, Queen's Bench Division*, vol. 14 (1884–85). (1985). London: William Clowes and Sons. In J. Arthur and W. H. Shaw (3rd ed.) *Readings in the Philosophy of Law.* Upper Saddle River, NJ: Prentice Hall, pp. 281–286.

Walzer, Michael. (1983). *Spheres of Justice: A Defense of Pluralism and Equality*. USA: Basic Books.

Abstract

This paper assesses the moral and legal plausibility of religious exemption statutes, which relieve parents of the obligation to seek medical care for their children due to religious beliefs. The public's connection to dissimilar doctrines is too distinct to allow them to become the basis for enduring political decisions. Thus, when the government makes a public policy regarding exemption statutes, it must do it using objective criterion. It should rank the interests of the groups involved including churches, parents, children and the state. A criterion of differentiating between the needs and desires of each group and placing them into a scale of relative urgency, proves to be a useful guide for assessing which groups' interest should be awarded the highest rank. I found that the government should repeal exemption statutes, allowing children's health interests to prevail and subsequently justified the conviction of parents for negligence if these laws are repealed.

REINSTATING GOVERNMENT NEUTRALITY: THE REPEAL OF RELIGIOUS EXEMPTION STATUTES

Sari Goldmeer

Introduction

The Supreme Court has addressed the First Amendment's free exercise clause to the Constitution throughout the decades. Some of their judgments are regarded as attacks on religious liberty, while others are praised as respecting the integrity of the clause. Even within the court, there is widespread disagreement as to the applied meaning of this clause due to its ambiguity. This article examines one of the most controversial issues that must be addressed by the highest court, the existence of religious exemption laws or statutes, relieving parents/legal guardians of the duty to seek medical care for their children due to religious beliefs. The constitutionality of these statutes has not yet been determined. However, a standardized means of ranking needs of urgency and growth of societal attitudes towards accepting distinct interests of children would provide the Supreme Court with a prudent rationale for repealing exemption laws.

Exemption Laws

In 1974, the U.S. Department of Health, Education and Welfare (HEW) enacted the Child Abuse Prevention and Treatment Act. HEW required states that receive child abuse prevention and treatment grants from the federal government to enact religious exemptions for child abuse and neglect charges (Massie 1994: 734). According to exemption laws, the state cannot currently intervene if parents medically treat their child as the tenets of their religion require. However, upon the child's death, medical immunity laws do not exempt parents from prosecution for criminal acts such as involuntary manslaughter and child endangerment for religious reasons (Definitions of Child Abuse and Neglect District of Columbia). Thus, there is an obvious inconsistency when spiritual exemption laws and manslaughter statutes are interpreted together. In many cases, parents have been able to elude criminal conviction due to the discrepancy between statutes for which they otherwise would have likely been convicted under CAPTA (Saroyan 2003: 363–387).

In 1996, Congress attempted to clarify the apparent discrepancy providing that states could "initiate legal proceedings in a court of competent jurisdiction, to provide medical care or treatment for a child with life threatening conditions" (Merrick 2003: 279). Despite this provision, most parents are often shielded from prosecution, arguing that state exemption laws led them to believe that the use of healing as a substitute for conventional medical care was condoned regardless of the treatment's outcome (Saroyan 2003: 363–387).

Interested parties have attempted to influence legislative regulations and policy decisions concerning exemption laws. Many religious sects have ardently lobbied legislators to support exemption statutes. Meanwhile, medical societies, governmental authorities and child advocacy groups have vehemently opposed spiritual exemption statutes all calling for repeal or re-provisions of the state exemption laws (Merrick 2003: 279–280). The arguments generate public interest as to the substance of the exemption laws themselves and whether parents have a right to withhold conventional medical treatment from their children on religious grounds.

In order to better comprehend the issues underlying this problem, it is necessary to examine four arguments regarding religious exemption laws. A moral standard will then be developed from which the needs and desires of the relevant parties can be evaluated. This standard will then allow me to assess the moral and legal plausibility of religious exemption laws, which present parents with the religious liberty to withhold medical treatment from their children, while shielding themselves from prosecution for negligence.

Standard of Relative Urgency

The existence of spiritual exemption laws creates a controversy in moral philosophy. Reasonable persons weigh values differently and reach distinct judgments, mostly in part due to their lifestyle choices, background and experiences[1] (Rawls 1993: 55). Particularly, within a democracy, the public's connection to dissimilar doctrines is too distinct to allow these views to be a foundation for an enduring and sensible political decision. In that governmental neutrality is the only way to sustain a stable and just society, the government's duty is to find a secular doctrine that derives legitimacy independently from ecclesiastical authority (xviii–xx). This undoubtedly requires promoting a moral theory that would serve to formulate public policy and legislation regarding exemption laws that citizens affirming reasonable yet distinct doctrines might support.

A criterion of differentiating between needs and desires of each group and placing them into a scale of relative urgency represents only one source of moral insight capable of appraising exemption statutes. However, it is well suited to formulate public policies and to weigh competing interests. This moral theory must undoubtedly utilize objective criterions, due to an inability to subjectively promote the interests of all without overriding urgent needs of others. Implicit in the definition of objective criterion is the idea that we must attach an impartial value to some interests at the cost of sacrificing or subordinating others while determining public policies.[2] Rather than rationally justifying an appraisal of exemption laws by appealing to one's individual preference, the relevant interests must be objectively placed into a "hierarchy of relative urgency" (Scanlon 1975: 660–661). Thus, the government must be forced to select among competing interests in order to sustain as a pluralistic society.

The distinction between urgent claims and non-urgent claims is related to a discussion of needs and desires. A desire is that which a person merely wants due to the fact that he feels it is advantageous but not necessary, such as taking a trip. A desire can form voluntarily or arise independently of a person's decisions (Frankfurt 1984: 8). On the contrary, needs often evoke a sense of urgency and claim of entitlement, as one cannot reach a particular end without a need. However, the mere fact that something is a necessity does not necessarily grant it more urgent moral consideration than a desire. For example, a person might wish to draw a picture and needs an instrument to draw. One can hardly assert that this person's need deserves more importance than any desire. This need is volitional in the sense that the person requires something only to satisfy a desire, specifically drawing. In this case, the person desired to draw voluntarily and decided what he required in order to fulfill this desire (2–4). Often, volitional needs arise due to particular comprehensive doctrines that individuals affirm. These needs are not respected by all individuals as advantageous tools that are necessary to pursue all conceptions of the good and should be awarded the same public status of relative urgency as desires.

Formulating policy decisions that advance non-volitional needs sanction ends that form independently of one's desires, notably goods that will permit a person to function and develop as a human being such as nutrition, shelter, sleep and health (Daniels 1981: 153–154). Non-volitional needs can be viewed as those basic instruments that all individuals require in order to pursue their personal conception of the good, despite philosophical, cultural and religious variations. Thus, an individual's claim to a non-volitional need appeals to an objective standard of species functioning rather than a standard based upon higher interests associated with subjective desires and preferences.

There appears to be a moral priority for fulfilling non-volitional needs before desires or volitional-needs. Admittedly, there are times when it is preferable for an individual to forgo a non-volitional need in exchange for something that he desires. To some individuals, the subjective value they would derive from fulfillment of their desires are worth more than the benefit they would derive from non-volitional needs. More specifically, an individual may wish to use spiritual healing to maintain his health, despite evidence that suggests it is not an effective means of treatment. Autonomous individuals should be permitted to determine their own standard of urgency according to the criteria they choose. An individual may assign an unusually high urgency status to any volitional need/desire within the confines of the law, but may not reduce non-volitional needs of another as a result. Without the former, an individual does not have the future ability to pursue the latter.

The aim of public policy is to respect competing conceptions of the good. Although the government should respect the advancement of individuals' volitional needs within confines of the law, those interests must not preclude the advancement of another individual's non-volitional needs (Rawls 1993: 183). By subsequently examining the interests of the four relevant parties affected by exemption laws, including *religious groups, parents, children and the state*, I shall discover which of these groups' interests is most urgent. I can then rank them in an effort to formulate government policy that will most effectively promote justice upon implementation.

Groups Espousing Alternative Healing Treatments

Theological principles and practices of religious groups espousing unorthodox methods of treating their ill children pose a moral dilemma to many outside of their fold. I intend these arguments to be applicable to all such recognized religious groups who espouse unconventional medical care in lieu of conventional medical care.

Christian Science Tradition

The Christian Science Church is the largest, most prominent religious group espousing unconventional medical treatment. Christian Scientists place spiritual insight as the supreme motivator in order to generate well-being and a harmonious relationship with God. Followers maintain that disease cannot exist because illness is physical, and there is no reality to physical matter. By relinquishing false thoughts and returning to spiritual reality, sickness vanishes (*Christian Science Sourcebook* 1990: 160–161).

Followers of Christian Science contact practitioners, who are lay members of the Church devoted to the practice of spiritual healing. The practitioner helps the ill patient to dismiss the illegitimate belief in disease. In treating children, practitioners focus on the remediation of the thoughts of their parents, since the minds of children are heavily influenced by the beliefs of parents (Gevitz 1991: 422–424). Followers believe that when an individual pursues conventional medical treatment, he implicitly rejects the power of prayer. Thus, prayer is not as potent when used simultaneously with medical treatment (Merrick 1994: 327–328). Clearly, this concept of treatment is based upon a different premise than that of mainstream society.

Fundamentalist Sects

There are at least twenty fundamentalist sects of mainstream religious groups in the United States who utilize prayer in lieu of conventional medical treatment. Although they all adhere to different theological principles, the Faith Assembly and the Followers of Christ Church are two of the most recognized groups.

FAITH ASSEMBLY DOCTRINE

Mainstream followers of the Faith Assembly assert that the rehabilitation efforts of Christ provide them with inspiration to heal through prayer. Fundamentalist adherents believe that use of conventional medicine and physicians are inconsistent with one's belief in divine healing. They believe that one rejects the power of faith healing and the power of Jesus by seeking medical treatment (Faith Assembly Church).

FOLLOWERS OF CHRIST CHURCH

Mainstream followers of Christ Church believe in a literal translation of the Scriptures. Like Christian Scientists, they view health in moralistic rather than biological terms. The fundamentalist followers firmly believe that elders must anoint individuals suffering from ailments and that faith can heal all illness, as required by the scriptures. Seeking medical treatment would put one's faith in man's hand rather than the hands of God, an irrational action on the part of a believer (Larabee).

Analysis of Empirical Evidence

Officials from all of the religious groups previously mentioned admit that despite their approach to healing, deaths among followers occasionally occur. However, Christian Scientists maintain that their methods of healing by prayer are as effective or superior to conventional medicine in healing all illnesses (Gevitz 1991: 433–444). Specifically, the Christian Science Church has presented its "healing record" by means of religious testimonies and anecdotal reports. Their study, titled "An Empirical Analysis of Medical Evidence in Christian Science Testimonies of Healing, 1969–1988" published over 10,000 testimonies of physical healing (DesAutels 1995: 104, note 18).

Opponents question the reliability of these testimonies. The testimonies provide no access to cited medical documentation, excluding the possibility of independently qualifying the claims. The reliability of testimonial claims is further undermined because many of the cited individuals failed to obtain diagnostic verification of illnesses that they reported. Without evidence, it is inconceivable to assume that recovery and use of prayer were causally related. Furthermore, it is also difficult to assess whether healed individuals would have recovered regardless, due to their body's natural resistance (Battin 1995: 115).

Thus, the question arises as to whether parents who have a different religious view of healing, have a right to withhold effective conventional medical treatment from their children. Until medical professionals have independently verified its effectiveness, the substitution of conventional medical practices for alternative faith healing should not be viewed as sufficient means of health care for children. In 1998, Pediatrician Dr. Seth Asser published a paper in the Journal Pediatrics that evaluated the deaths of 172 children, who died between 1975 and 1995 from families of twenty three religious groups. One hundred and forty suffered from illnesses for which survival rates with medical care would have surpassed 90% (Asser and Swan 1998: 625–629).

I am not arguing that effective methods of medical treatment do not exist outside of conventional western medicine. However, the validity of these studies is questionable unless the results can be replicated by subsequent studies using larger samples for greater reliability. As of yet, religious groups have been unwilling to participate in comprehensive comparative studies, arguing that mental states cannot be observed in controlled settings and it would be spiritually destructive to undergo conventional diagnosis (Battin 1995: 115–116). Thus, it is reasonable to assert that we should rely on the only current truth available at this time, conventional medical treatment, to treat minor children. Only when religious groups or other individuals claiming the effectiveness of intercessory prayer subject their healing practices to rigorous studies, can medical science begin to investigate the merit of spiritual healing as an "adequate treatment," as guaranteed by the 1983 modified provision of CAPTA.[3]

The previously discussed religious groups are characterized by the fundamental belief that spiritual healing is an effective means of medical treatment. They have a volitional need for the government to condone spiritual healing and exemption statutes in order to fulfill a desire. Thus, the fulfillment of this need is related to a specific, subjective comprehensive doctrine. These groups play a role in helping to secure the benefits of religious freedom to their followers and fostering religious acceptance in pluralistic societies. Church leaders would be burdened upon repeal of exemption laws, as they would be forced to make radical changes in their religious practices. Compulsory medical treatment for minors would force the churches to reconcile the fact that their tenets conflict with human laws. More importantly, they would be forced to do this without losing their followers' confidence in the stability of the church's tenets. However, theoretically, questioning religious beliefs and practices does not invariably endanger their stability. Parents would still be able to use spiritual healing as a means of treatment, thus showing their children the lifestyle they could one day choose to accept. The other alternative available to the church is to succumb to analysis, attempting to prove that spirituality is an adequate medical treatment that should be protected by exemption laws.

These burdens do not warrant the same level of urgency awarded to a non-volitional need. A standard of relative urgency must award priority to those needs concerning virtually everyone and are necessary for functioning. A church appeal for exemptions essentially requests a public policy to urgently prioritize their volitional need to advance spiritual healing despite the fact that it is not a need that can be affirmed by individuals holding different values. The logical public priority should not unfairly diminish an individual's goods, which aid in his non-volitional species functioning, while another group pursues higher interests. The basic structure of this society is built in a way that encourages citizens to affirm public policies independent of one's own conception of the good. However, the religious group's need still must be considered in relation to the three subsequent interests to determine its level of urgency.

Parental Rights Approaches

Evaluating parental rights claims will allow me to demonstrate that their claims cannot outweigh interests of children on the scale of urgency. One component to the parental rights approach is based upon the premise that it is a parent's privilege to raise his children according to his own standards. The other claim is that it is a parent's right to religious liberty as protected by the First Amendment to provide his children with religious healing treatments according to the tenets of his religion.

Parental Autonomy

Respect for parental autonomy is a morally defensible argument put forth by Church officials to justify parental responsibility for the care of the child. Philosophers, Allen E. Buchanan and Dan W. Brock justify the right of a parent to serve as their child's surrogate decision maker. They concede that parents possess the right to raise their children according to any values they deem appropriate, presumably care for the child's well-being and bear the consequences of their child's treatment. However, Buchanan and Brock admit that these arguments are plausible only to the extent to which the child's well-being coincides with that of his parents (232–234). Thus, the parental rights arguments are adequate to justify parental guidance, but the rights of parenthood are not beyond the limitation of state interference.

I propose that the role of a parent should be regarded as analogous to that of a trustee. By definition, a trustee is "a person or one of a group of persons responsible for the property or affairs of another person or of an institution, business firm, or the like" ("Trustee" def. 1). This conception of parental rights implies that a parent should hold the right to exercise authority over his child and his child's interests. Parents must govern their children until they develop the reasoning and capacity to govern themselves.[4] This influence cannot be unlimited, but must be viewed as temporary authority to aid in the instruction and welfare of their offspring.

Although an autonomous man is clearly different from a child, the analogy must be considered in order to illustrate a particular argument about a trustee relationship. Inherent in the definition of trustee is the assumption that the owner of "an institution, business firm, or the like" will be autonomous, but not intellectually proficient in making specialized decisions. Suppose a financial advisor was delegated authority to invest a man's funds for future. This man lacks specialized financial knowledge and the advisor assumed the role of his trustee. The man discovered that the advisor placed his money in unusually high-risk stocks, as he believed it would be the best course of action, despite lack of empirical data to substantiate the advisor's confidence in the stock. It seems likely that society would accept the claim that the man can dismiss his trustee based on his well-intentioned but empirically risky decision that jeopardized his interests.

Similarly, if a parent does not fulfill his duties as trustee and fails to be responsible for the child's basic interests, the state should intervene and restrict the parents' actions, as is done in secular cases whereby parent neglect a child. By repealing exemption laws and adopting the standard set in neglect cases, the state can intervene under CAPTA, to prevent child neglect and to prosecute parents who fail to provide adequately for their children.

In order to avoid infringing upon parents who have compelling reasons to be decision makers, intervention should be limited to actions that fail to promote the child's basic interests rather than their best interests.[5] Suppose a Muslim parent will not allow his son to attend baseball practice on Fridays because it interferes with prayer at the mosque. This prohibition may limit this child from becoming a professional baseball player but does not undermine the child's basic interests. Parental rights should not be infringed upon to provide a quality of life advantage to the child but to protect their basic non volitional interests.

Parental claims for supporting exemption laws appeal to their volitional need to control the medical treatment and religious upbringing of their children. Satisfying these needs will fulfill their desire to provide for the spiritual well-being of their children. Sacrificing this need would pose a significant burden to parents based upon their specific hierarchy of relative urgency. However, parents can still help their children to acquire attitudes favoring spirituality notably through spiritual education. By using a subjective standard, the parents would designate the interest of providing their children with spiritual healing a ranking of supreme urgency. However, this need is one that directly corresponds with a certain comprehensive doctrine that others might not affirm.

Although the government should allow individual's to pursue their own doctrines, for those beliefs that potentially harm others, the government must interfere. As it has been biologically proven that aspects of health sustain human life, public policy must reflect the non-volitional needs of individuals to be satisfied rather than improperly distribute benefits to a particular conception of the good. Thus, although parents possess significant volitional interests, they cannot yet be assigned a ranking that would subordinate non-volitional physical needs of others.

Parental Free Exercise Rights

Advocates for religious exemption laws maintain that the parental rights approach also appears to find philosophical support in the free exercise clause of the Constitution's First Amendment, stating, "*Congress shall make no law respecting an establishment of religion or prohibiting the free exercise thereof*" (US Const., Amendment 1). Church officials have asserted that the Supreme Court case, *Wisconsin v. Yoder*, grants them the right to serve as their child's sole surrogate decision maker. In this case, the Court found Amish children could not be forced to attend school past eighth grade, as to prevent the state from intruding into the family and preventing parents from instilling their faith in their children, despite their interest in educating the children (*State of Wisconsin v. Yoder*). The context of the argument does not lend credence to the view that this line of reasoning is applicable in cases of medical treatment. One can reasonably presume that the state's interest in preserving the health and welfare of children constitutes a legitimate concern that may override a parent's free exercise claim. Thus, the majority decision would not likely apply in the case of medical treatment. The consequences of the parent's actions on a child are more debilitating than in the Yoder case, including death and permanent injury. This line of reasoning, placing the state's interest in the welfare of a child ahead of the free exercise claim, was employed in the United States Supreme Court case, *Prince v. Massachusetts*. In this case the parents' religious beliefs required that their children sell religious tracts in violation of child labor laws. The Court ruled "parents may be free to become martyrs themselves. But it does not follow they are free, in identical circumstances, to make martyrs of their children before they have reached the age of full legal discretion when they can make that choice for themselves." It seems to follow that the court would not accept the claim that parents are at liberty to allow their child to be exposed to "ill health or death" (*Prince v. Commonwealth of Massachusetts*). The Court regards the welfare of a child as an interest of the highest order and would override the legitimate claims to the free exercise of religion.

Upon evaluating both parental rights claims, it is apparent that parents have a volitional need invested in their desire to maintain religious exemption laws. A parent's free exercise claim qualifies as a volitional need, as it is not necessary for species functioning. Granted, the preservation of this interest concerns virtually everyone, even a secular individual. The exercise claim allows for a pluralistic society that promotes toleration, an ideal which facilitates a society of cooperating agents. However, the clause does not grant parental interests a status of supreme urgency. Allowing religious doctrines to guide behavior would permit religious beliefs to override government's role and "in effect to permit every citizen to become a law unto himself" (*Reynolds v. U.S.*). Governmental imposition would not force parents to abandon precepts of their religion but prevent parents from using those precepts to endanger the non-volitional needs of others.

Children's Basic Interests

Children have interests despite ongoing arguments that a child should not be awarded the same moral status as an adult. I do not think this premise is well supported, but for the sake of argument, I will adopt the view that children should be treated differently from adults. Thus, I will not presuppose that a child's basic interests are the end values of human life. Throughout this article, the terms "basic interests" and "best interests" have been referenced. It is necessary to clarify these terms to analyze limitations on parental rights with full understanding.

Basic interests that children possess should be characterized in three ways: (1) inherent right to life, which include goods that are instrumental to their basic physical interests, including medical care (2) right to goods which aid in their intellectual, and emotional development (3) what Joel Feinberg refers to as a "right to an open future" (Miller 2003: 41). A child's right to an open future should be defined as "rights in trust," also referred to as C-rights. Thus, "the right to an open future" is the right against a premature violation, which would result in a child's inability to exercise his future class A-rights, such as protected liberties and rights, which belong solely to adults (Feinberg 1980: 124–153). When children become adults, they should have the option to practice their chosen religion. There is no guarantee that the children who died in absence of medical treatment would have adhered to the principles of their parents' religion, had they lived to exercise their rights.

The above "basic interests" are merely goods children need in order to pursue life's more comprehensive goods. The use of the term "basic interests" is not associated with any particular conception of the good life (Miller 2003: 41–42). For argument's sake, the child is not entitled to, nor does he have a claim rights that exceed those listed. However, by accepting this claim, we must recognize that a child's well-being does not solely rest on a parent's volition but must be evaluated by principles of governmental neutrality constructed to protect the basic interests of children.

As the child has not yet reached the age at which he can employ his own hierarchy of relative urgency, it is difficult to balance their interests with those of the other relevant interests. Children, like all members of society have a supreme interest in their physical well-being. Without physical well-being, one's development would be severely hindered. Children born into religious homes should be granted the basic capacities necessary to form their own conceptions of the good. Without a repeal of the legislation, the children will receive empirically unsubstantiated treatments. Prioritizing volitional needs over non-volitional health needs would invariably devalue the child imposing a potentially debilitating doctrine upon him.

Parens Patriae

In accordance with the doctrine, *Parens Patriae*, the state retains the right to restrict parental decision-making authority when parental behavior threatens a child's welfare. The government has a compelling interest in the welfare of minors, insofar as it will promote the healthy growth of young people into citizens. Governmental interest often justifies restrictive regulations for the physical well-being of its citizens (*Prince v. Massachusetts*). Thus, the state must sufficiently satisfy the objective, non-volitional health needs of its youngest citizens in order to grant the child the ability to enjoy a reasonable range of opportunities from which to choose their life pursuits.

The government should create policies that ensure citizens maintain goods to minimally satisfy the non-volitional needs of everyone, prior to allowing individuals to pursue higher volitional interests. After all, its position is one influencing the principles of justice and the future of pluralistic democracy. Therefore, the government must use principles independent of any particular view of the good. In application, this requires the government to repeal exemption laws to secure the most fundamental aspect of human life, health.

Implementation of Urgency Standard

After evaluating the four arguments, conflict between relevant parties is clearly expected. To find a common basis for assessing urgent needs and desires, I outlined a theory that advances a standard independent of a particular comprehensive doctrine. It attempts to satisfy those needs that develop before most individuals can adequately pursue their vision of the good. This standard does not criticize moral judgments of religiously motivated groups. Rather it is constructed as part of a secular doctrine comprised of ideals based on principles of practical reason rather than ecclesiastical reason (Rawls 1993: xx).

According to current empirical truth, a person's ability to pursue his comprehensive doctrine relies upon the fulfillment of his non-volitional needs. Only once they are fulfilled can an individual create his own conceptions of the good (188). Of course, he can choose to sacrifice his non-volitional need for that which he feels would benefit him more. However, the standard of relative urgency requires that volitional needs cannot be imposed upon a minor child until their urgent non-volitional needs are satisfied. The family and religious groups are units subject to state regulation, despite their claim of possessing religious liberty. The state must ensure that children's development is protected in order for them to reach the point at which they too can decide what gives meaning and value to their lives. In the case of religious exemption laws, the state's central interest parallels the child's non-volitional need. Thus, it is not necessary to balance competing claims.[6]

As illness can be debilitating and the use of spiritual healing would possibly heighten that risk for the child, it is vital that their health interest remains one of superior urgency to a volitional need or desire. The best course of action would be for the government to repeal exemption laws, thus implicitly mandating medical treatment within a limited period of time. This would treat all children as equal under the law and not absolve parents from their duty to provide for their child's health interests. However, until exemption laws are repealed or modified, many parents still face criminal charges and are brought to trial upon their child's death. If exemption laws are repealed and a parent withholds conventional medical treatment, he would instead face charges for negligence while the child is alive. Although we have examined the reasons why the child's interests should be placed above the others on the scale of relative urgency, it is necessary to justify convicting parents for negligence once exemption laws are repealed.

Moral Culpability

In order to establish whether a parent who withholds medical treatment from his child is legally responsible for his negligent behavior, it is necessary to evaluate moral responsibility. It is often difficult to regard an action taken in good faith as one that should be subject to legal prosecution. However, finding one morally culpable will rationalize the potential finding of legal liability.

An essential distinction to examine is doing harm and allowing harm. Some assume these two are conceptually distinct. Doing harm is the act of creating a threat that would not have existed independently of the agent's conduct and is generally regarded as an action for which people are morally culpable. On the contrary, allowing harm does not create a threat because the victim is already under a threat (Norcross). An agent's deeds can be characterized as either interventions in a natural process or abstentions from intervention. Jonathan Bennett attempts to evaluate this argument by examining a morally neutral example. He centers his discussion on a pair of cases involving an unoccupied car rolling off a cliff. In the case "Push," an agent pushes a stationary car, "making" it roll off the cliff to its destruction. In the other case "Stayback," the car is already rolling towards the edge of the cliff. The agent could prevent it from falling by placing a rock or boulder in its path but he does not, allowing it to be destroyed (Bennett 1993: 230–240). Many philosophers suppose that beneficence, or an act done to benefit others and further their legitimate interests is more of an altruistic ideal than an obligation (Beauchamp and Childress 2001: 167). They suppose that placing the rock in the car's path is an ideal action, not an obligatory one. Thus, the agent who failed to act would not be morally culpable. In terms of general beneficence it can be argued that an act done to benefit others should be viewed as an ideal one. Although it is debatable, for the purposes of this discussion, moral culpability is attached only to doing harm and is absent from allowing harm to occur, when referring to general beneficence.

When the case involves people with whom you have special relations, I find the distinction between doing and allowing harm is not always morally significant. We have different obligations to people with whom we are in close interpersonal relationships, rather than those with whom we have no relationship. A specific duty to perform a beneficent action arises in cases of special relationships. Ties between family and close friends create determinate obligations that rest on special moral relations or commitments.

Individuals do not have these obligatory commitments to the general public (174–175).

Perhaps this discussion would be better clarified by evaluating Philosopher, Peter Singer's argument. Singer defends the concept of extending moral obligations. He contends "if it is in our power to prevent something bad from happening, without thereby sacrificing something of comparable moral importance, we ought, morally, to do it" (Singer qtd. in Arthur 2002: 310). Adopting Singer's view requires the agent to act in ways that some might consider beyond moral obligations, in other words, moral ideals. The moral obligation to disrupt our life plans in order to benefit those in need is not clear in a case of general beneficence. Whether Singer's proposal is an ideal or an obligation of general beneficence, many individuals accept this standard as one of common morality that often guides behavior. Thus, if this standard serves as a common guide to general beneficence, responsibilities that individuals have to those people with whom they are in special relationships must exceed the Singer's standard.

In cases of special beneficence, failing to act in ways that prevent and remove harm to others is morally deficient, as there is a clear obligation to help. Morality demands more obligations to those with whom we have special moral relations that "stem not only from interpersonal encounters, but from settled rules, roles, and relations that constitute the matrix of social obligations and role derived obligations" (Beauchamp and Childress 2001: 174–175). Even religiously motivated parents and religious groups would adopt a proposed principle that heightened their moral obligations to their loved ones. Thus, Singer's principle requires slight modification, so that "*if it is in our power to prevent something bad from happening, using reasonably sound means, without thereby sacrificing something of comparable moral importance, we ought, morally, to do it.*" Thus, this principle should heighten the morally obligatory actions for individuals involved in special relationships.

Once it is determined that a parent has a moral obligation to help his child according to the guidelines set forth by the modified Singer principle, it is important to determine whether or not the parent is morally culpable for withholding conventional medical treatment from his children. Breaching one's special beneficent duty to prevent harm, established by the modified Singer principle, may be as wrong as one's intentionally doing the harm.

By putting aside our preconceived perceptions of sensitive terminology, we can evaluate the moral difference of doing and allowing harm in the case of a parent withholding conventional medical treatment from his child. Allowing harm can be seen as abstaining from an act and allowing what would have happened independently of one's intervention. It could also be seen as preventing a person from being helped[7] (Hanser 1999: 277–295).

Although preventing someone from being assisted appears to be more negatively charged than abstaining from aiding a harmed individual, both should still categorized as allowing harm. One cannot rationally conclude that a religiously motivated parent who withholds medical treatment from his child is doing harm. The parent did not inflict initial threat upon the child. Therefore, the actions of the parent must fall into one of the two subsets under the category of "allowing harm." One cannot characterize the parent's actions as abstention because it is assumed they act in good faith by engaging in help seeking behavior. However, they are imposing unverified healing upon their children, excluding medically proven treatments that are available. Thus, the actions of the parent appear to fall under the category of preventing someone from being helped from harm.

In one case, preventing people from being saved from harm could be construed to mean that an individual had malevolent motives, and deliberately prevented the individual from being helped. However, this concept need not be associated with malicious intentions. Certainly, in our discussion of faith healers, the parent's motives are far from malevolent. "Preventing people from being helped from harm" could also be construed to mean that an individual in a special relationship, who given many sound choices, excludes the option that would most likely have a more favorable result. If this is the case, doing harm should not be regarded as morally worse than allowing harm to occur. Therefore, this interpretation does not exclude the fact that an agent could have acted in a positive way with benevolent motives, but their action was not sufficient to guarantee a sound result.

Specifically, in the case of religiously motivated parents, there are alternate ways in which they could act, aside from their dependence on the unreliable power of prayer. Thus, to assess moral culpability in the case of special relations, I propose exercising the sound alternative principle: *When an individual has multiple options available, some of which are sound, and ex-*

cludes an option with a record of achieving probable success, he is morally culpable. There is a chance that spiritual healing could in fact be viewed as a sound treatment. However, until it is determined valid, I assume it is not a sound treatment capable of producing benefits comparable to that of conventional medicine. This discussion does not exclude the possibility that a parent can choose to employ an experimental, risky medical treatment for his child, assuming that there are not sound treatments available that have a similar record of achieving success. Similarly, a parent may choose among available treatments within the confines of proven, orthodox treatments. A sound treatment need only meet the child's "basic interests," so it is not necessary that a parent choose a treatment that may result in greater net benefits. However, if an agent excludes a sound means of action, when sound ones are available, the moral distinction between doing and allowing harm appears to be an insignificant one.

Once it is determined that a parent had a moral obligation to help his child, due to guidelines surrounding special beneficence, the sound alternative principle must be evoked in order to establish moral culpability. Granted, individuals should balance an action's benefits by weighing any comparable risks or significant incurred costs to themselves. Referencing the discussion of the relative standard of urgency will demonstrate that as a public policy, the volitional need of a parent cannot qualify as a comparable moral cost that outweighs the non-volitional needs of a child.

Within this new context, it is necessary to reevaluate and modify Jonathan Bennett's examples. Suppose an agent could probably prevent the car from falling by placing a boulder in its path. However, by placing a rock in its path, the car is just as likely, or more likely to fall than it would by placing the boulder in its path. It seems reasonable to assert that a parent who chose the rock rather than the boulder would be morally culpable. Spiritual healing cannot represent the boulder, as a boulder is empirically proven to be a more effective shield than a rock. Although religiously motivated parents can theoretically presume spiritual healing is a more effective shield, currently, empirical evidence proves it is representative of the rock. By pursuing a potentially unsound means of treatment, a parent who withholds a sound treatment from his child is preventing that child from receiving help. That prevention must therefore be regarded as morally on a par with doing harm.

Legal Liability

We are presented with an apparent contradiction in that religiously motivated parents are morally culpable for an action they did not wish to occur. Admittedly, religiously motivated parents genuinely believe in the soundness of spiritual healing. However, a parent has a special duty to investigate the soundness of this belief when an action stemming from this belief will affect his child. If a reasonable parent would recognize that it is within his power to prevent something bad from happening by using the sound means of treatment, then the parent who employs an unverified treatment, while conventional ones are available, is morally and legally culpable (Clifford 1999: 238–240). To predict the degree of responsibility, a religiously motivated parent should be judged according to the standards of any reasonable person, that of a cautious individual. The reasonable person makes an effort to be appropriately informed, capable, aware of the law and fair-minded (Prosser qtd. in Arthur 2001: 399).

A crucial question that must be considered is whether a reasonable person would withhold conventional medical treatment from his child based on the available evidence. A reasonable parent would be aware of the empirically proven conventional medical treatment. He would seek to provide for his child's basic interests, independently of his own values. After all, as a reasonable person, he would be aware that that a society permitting each individual to act upon his own conscience, cannot sustain. If the parent is socialized in a society whereby conventional treatment is the only proven means of care, he has an obligation not to exclude that form of treatment. One cannot overlook the fact that the parent was under both a legal and moral duty to provide for the child.

Guiding Public Policy

Exemption laws essentially allow religiously motivated individuals to follow different standards from the rest of society. Different members of society would be subject to different standards of liability, leading to inequality within the justice system. Taking subjective values into account would in turn undermine "the reasonable expectations of members of the community," possibly depreciating the standards of care that the community reasonably expects (Stepniak). Additionally, any honorable interpretation of the establishment clause could not possibly conclude that a state's exemption of a religious group from legal responsibility, in an otherwise prosecutable offense (child neglect), is not granting special preference to one religion. Consequently, it is paradoxical that religious exemption laws seem to breach the establishment clause.

When a child is suffering from a life threatening illness, most state laws stipulate that a medical doctor must be consulted (Child Abuse Prevention and Treatment and Adoption Reform Act). However, critically ill children of certain religious sects are exempt from scrutiny by outside powers until it is too late to prevent a disastrous outcome (Swan 1998–1999: 73–95). It is preferable to preclude the death of a child by permitting state intervention. However, this requires change in public policy through the repeal of exemption laws.

Religious exemption laws are unjust because they rob these children of the essential right to a healthy life via medical treatment, which the government ensures to other children. Repealing exemption laws is necessary to ensure that these children obtain the equivalent legal statutes of health care granted to other children by CAPTA. All laws involved with child abuse, child neglect and medical neglect must be followed, allowing no exemption for religious sects. If the current system of exemptions remains in practice, then we must continue to face the dilemma of prosecuting parents for involuntary manslaughter. The previous observation that parents employing spiritual healing do not willfully neglect the child, has been the main factor discouraging state action in terms of prosecution. By repealing exemption laws the government could likely save the lives of ill children, prosecuting parents who do not comply with CAPTA, invariably mandating conventional medical treatment. This seems to be a more prudent option than charging parents with involuntary manslaughter after the unfortunate death of their children.

Conclusion

This article has examined philosophical issues relevant to any discussion of religious exemption laws. The arguments presented must be thoroughly considered by a higher court of law. The repeal of exemption laws is essentially a proposal for government neutrality to reinstate the necessary constitutional neutrality between government and religious adherents as intended by the First Amendment. Government intervention should be viewed as promoting the repeal of a governmental imposed burden on children born into these religious homes. Granted, by repealing exemption laws, the Supreme Court or another higher court would leave religious sects vulnerable to prosecution under neglect laws, which inevitably would involve government interference. However, government would be serving its original, legitimate purpose, that of preserving the equal protection of all its citizens.

Notes

1 Reasonable persons are defined as "those who have realized their two moral powers to a degree sufficient to be free and equal citizens in a constitutional regime, and who have an enduring desire to honor fair terms of cooperation and to be fully cooperating members of society."

2 This method of assessment is discussed by Scanlon in "Preference and Urgency," pp. 658–659. This criterion could account for social relativism and allows for the possibility that a policy or institution would impose different benefits and burdens on different people. The objective criterion does not exclude the importance of accounting for subjective interests. For example, considering individual preferences when formulating social policy, could be a primary objective value.

3 See the legislation, C.F.R. § 1340.2 (d) (2) (ii) (1993) for a clear definition of "adequate treatment."

4 Determinations about a child's competence to make medical decisions vary. Any attempt to limit the wishes of the autonomous patient would be unjustifiably paternalistic. Thus, the age at which a person is fully competent to make his own medical treatment decision should not be fixed. Relying on ages in set classes in regards to decisions concerning one's own medical care, disregards each child's individual competency. We must not assign minors the formidable task of making treatment decisions they cannot decide rationally. On the other hand, we cannot deny this opportunity to those individuals who are fully capable. It is best left up to the courts to determine individually, the age at which a specific individual becomes an "autonomous patient." A psychologist should be consulted in order to decide whether a particular child is capable of self determination. In part, this decision should be based upon the depth of a child's deliberations and their cognitive and intellectual capacities.

5 Buchanan and Brock identify the Best Interest Standard as one that requires a determination of the net benefit of each possible option available to the patient. Designating a net benefit to each option entails determining the degree to which each of the options would further specific interests. One must then subtract any possible costs or detriments incurred from the benefits of each option. Thus, one cannot determine that a treatment which merely benefits the patient would be in his best interests, until the possible costs are calculated as well. Employing other possible treatments may result in greater net benefits to the patient, or alternatively, the costs of action could subtract from the overall value of the benefits. Such benefits and burdens would specifically address how a treatment option affects that patient's life. Decisions about treatment options, which address the character of one's life and the worth of one's life, inevitably involve quality of life judgments (122–123).

6 In cases whereby multiple non-volitional needs conflict, it would be necessary to determine which interests rank as more critical on the objective scale of relative urgency. In creating a scale, it would be valuable to consult Rawls' *Political Liberalism*, as he uses neutral principles independent of a particular comprehensive doctrine.

7 The idea of preventing people from being saved has been modified to preventing people from being helped in this article. Hanser adds this concept to that of killing and letting die to serve as an additional group. He affirms that preventing someone from being saved is morally equivalent to letting die. I object to his explanation that preventing someone from being saved does not appeal to the violation of the right to continued life as does killing. Rather, he believes that it appeals to the violation to the right to life saving aid similarly to letting die. It is difficult to accept the assumption that the former is morally worse than the latter for the reasons I affirm. Additionally, I include the concept of preventing someone from being harmed under the category of letting die. However, even if I would have accepted his argument that preventing someone from being saved is a separate category, I would have arrived at the same conclusion.

Works Cited

Asser, Seth and Rita Swan. "Child Fatalities from Religion Motivated Medical Neglect," *Pediatrics* 101.4 (April 1998), pp. 625–629.

Battin, Margaret. P. (1995). "Put Up or Shut Up? A Reply to Peggy Desatuel's Defense of Christian Science," *Journal of Social Philosophy* 26.3: 113–122.

Beauchamp, Tom L. and James F. Childress. (2001). *Principles of Biomedical Ethics Fifth Edition.* Oxford: Oxford University Press.

Bennett, Jonathan. (1994). "Negation and Abstention: Two Theories of Allowing." *Killing and Letting Die*. Ed. Bonnie Steinbeck and Alaister Norcross. New York: Fordham University Press, pp. 230–256.

Buchanan, Allen E. and Dan W. Brock. (1989). *Deciding for Others: Ethics of Surrogate Decision Making*. Cambridge: Cambridge University Press.

Child Abuse Prevention and Treatment Act. 31 January 1974. Pub. L. No. 93-47, 88 Stat. 4.

Child Abuse Prevention and Treatment and Adoption Reform Act. 26 January 1983. Pub. L No. 95-266. 92 Stat 205.

Christian Science Sourcebook of Contemporary Materials. (1990). Boston: Christian Science Publishing Society.

Clifford, W. K. "The Ethics of Belief." (1999). *Faith and Reason,* Ed. Paul Helm. Oxford: Oxford University Press.

Daniels, Norman. (1981). "Health Care and Distributive Justice," *Philosophy and Public Affairs* 10.2 (Spring): 146–179.

Definitions of Child Abuse and Neglect District of Columbia. (2001). D.C. Code Ann. §16-2301(9).

DesAutels, Peggy. (1995). "Christian Science, Rational Choice, and Alternative World Views," *Journal of Social Philosophy* 26.3 (Winter): 89–104.

Faith Assembly Church. (2003). "Seven Sermons" and "Reverend Raymond Jackson." 20 December 2003. http://www.fachurch.org/.

Feinberg, Joel. (1980). "The Child's Right to an Open Future." *Whose Child? Children's Rights, Parental Autonomy and State Power.* Ed. William Aiken and Hugh LaFollette. Totowa, NJ: Littlefield, Adams.

Frankfurt, Harry. (1984). "Necessity and Desire," *Philosophy and Phenomenological Research* 45.1 (September): 1–13.

Gevitz, Norman. (1991). "Christian Science Healing and the Health Care of Children," *Perspectives in Biology and Medicine* 34. 3 (Spring): 421–438.

Hanser, Matthew, (1999). "Killing, Letting Die and Preventing People from Being Saved," *Utilitas* 11.3 (November): 277–295.

Larabee, Mark. (1998). "Doubt, Secrecy Circle Followers of Christ." *The Oregonian*. 28 June 1998. 5 January 2004. http://www.rickross.com/reference/foc/foc1.html.

Massie, MacLean Ann. (1994). "The Religious Clauses and Parental Health Care Decisionmaking for Children: Suggestions for a New Approach," *Hastings Constitutional Law Quarterly* 21.3: 725–775.

Merrick, Janna. (1994). "Christian Science Healing of Minor Children: Spiritual Exemption Statutes, First Amendment Rights, and Fair Notice," *Issues in Law and Medicine* 10.3: 321–342.

———. (2003). "Spiritual Healing, Sick Kids and the Law: Inequities in the American Healthcare System," *American Journal of Law and Medicine* (Summer–Fall) 29(2–3): 269–299.

Miller, Richard B. (2003). *Children, Ethics, and Modern Medicine.* Bloomington: Indiana University Press.

Norcross, Alaister. (2002). "Killing and Letting Die." *The Blackwell Companion to Applied Ethics.* 11 November 2003. http://www.ruf.rice.edu/~norcross/Killingand LettingDie.pdf.

Prince v. Commonwealth of Massachusetts. No. 98. Supreme Ct. of the U.S. 31 January 1944.

Prosser, William. (2001). "Negligence." *Readings in the Philosophy of Law*, Third Edition. Ed. John Arthur and William H. Shaw. Upper Saddle River, NJ: Prentice Hall.

Rawls, John. (1993). *Political Liberalism.* New York: Columbia University Press.

Reynolds v. United States. No. Supreme Ct. of the U.S. 5 May 1879.

Saroyan, Zaven. (2003). "Spiritual Healing and the Free Exercise Clause: An Argument for the Use of Strict Scrutiny," *Boston University Public Interest Law Journal* 2–3: 363–387.

Scanlon, T. M. (1975). "Preference and Urgency," *Journal of Philosophy* 77: 655–669.

Singer, Peter. (2002). "Rich and Poor." *Morality and Moral Controversies: Readings in Moral, Social, and Political Philosophy,* Sixth Edition. Ed. John Arthur. Upper Saddle River, NJ: Prentice Hall.

State of Wisconsin v. Jonas Yoder, Wallace Miller, and Adin Yutz. No. 70-110. Supreme Ct. of the U.S. 15 May 1972.

Stepniak, Daniel. "Minority Values & the Reasonable Person of Torts," *Australasian Law Teachers Association 50th Anniversary Conference: Cross Currents: Internationalism, National Identity & Law.* 1995. 13 November 2003. http://bar.austlii.edu.au/au/special/alta/alta95/stepniak.html.

Swan, Rita. "Moral, Economic, and Social Issues in Children's Health Care: On Statutes Depriving a Class of Children's Rights to Medical Care: Can this Discrimination be Litigated?" *Quinnipiac Health Law* (1998–1999): 73–95.

"Trustee" *Worldbook Dictionary.* Vol. 2. (1993). Ed. Clarence L. Barnhart and Robert K. Barnhart. Chicago: William H. Nault Publishing.

Abstract

This paper explores a specific theory of judicial interpretation called original meaning. The theory's most vocal proponent has been Associate Justice Antonin Scalia. Judges who follow originalism remain loyal to the original meaning of the Constitution by ensuring that judges are restrained from making law based on personal predilections or biases that impair their judicial decisions. I will first explore whether originalism is historically congruent with a theory of interpretation that the "Framers" of the American Constitution envisioned. This paper will additionally present an alternative theory of interpretation called the empowerment principle, which permits judges to make law based on a theory of interpretation that protects the constitutional rights of the American people regardless of whether or not those principles are specifically written into the Constitution.

Justice Antonin Scalia argues that originalism is the best theory of constitutional interpretation because it prevents judges from "legislating from the bench," a phrase coined to describe how judges have overturned law thereby making new law. This paper will not argue that judges should be permitted to undermine the legislative branch of government by changing laws they feel are personally wrong. However, the concept of judges legislating from the bench is not as bad as it sounds. When a law that so egregiously undermines our constitutional principles goes unchanged by the legislature for decades, it may be appropriate for a judge to make new law.

THE STING OF ORIGINALISM: DEFENDING LEGISLATING FROM THE BENCH

Remington A. Gregg

Overview

This paper seeks to answer two questions: Is originalism the best way for judges to carry out their duties, and if not, how can one overcome the proposition that non-originalism is subjective and subjugates the role of the legislature, which is explicitly given the power to make law. In this pursuit, this paper will explore how two different sides of the philosophical spectrum interpret judicial review. Three important concepts, however, must be explained before going any further—the concept of judicial review, and theories of interpreting the Constitution through interpretevism (originalism) and non-interpretevism (non-originalism).

The principle of judicial review was conceived by John Marshall, the nation's fourth chief justice, in the majority opinion *Marbury v. Madison*. The crux of his opinion asserts that each branch of government—the national and state governments—are all enumerated with separate and distinct powers.

Second, the Bill of Rights protects the individual rights of citizen's against unwarranted actions of the federal and state governments. When such protections are breached, a person has the right to bring a suit against either the state or federal government. Third, it is the judiciary that decides whether that person has been wronged. Finally—and this is important to our supposition—when either the federal or state governments act constitutionally, their judgment, and not the Court's, must prevail. But, when the Supreme Court or a lower court finds that a person's rights were violated, the judgment of that Court prevails. This is called judicial review.

John Hart Ely, in his book, "Democracy and Distrust," categorizes theories of interpretation into two sides: interpretivism and noninterpretivism. Interpretivism argues that judges should confine themselves to enforcing norms that are "stated or clearly implicit in the written Constitution," (Ely 1980: 1) while noninterpretetivism argues that courts can and should go beyond these sets of norms when the specific law cannot be "discovered within the four corners of the document" (Ely 1980: 1). What separates these two theories for Ely is that judges who rely on an interpretivist theory of adjudication will only invalidate a law when an expressed or implicit prohibition is "fairly discoverable" (Ely 1980: 2) within the confines of the Constitution. This serves to limit the amount of judicial discretion judges can use.

Originalism is a misleading term because it has neither one main advocate, nor a principle doctrine. Under the heading of originalism are several theories of adjudication including original meaning, original intent and strict construction. Scalia does not advocate original intent because it can be too subjective. A strict construction, or interpretation, of the Constitution is a "degraded" (Scalia 1997: 23) form of originalism advocated most famously by President Richard Nixon. Other proponents of originalism are, or have been, Robert Bork, Edward Meese and William Rehnquist.[1] Our focus is on Antonin Scalia's theory of constitutional interpretation—original meaning—which has gone through many revisions in the last twenty years. There are few scholarly works on Scalia's originalism, and few official explications from the Justice. Nevertheless, this paper tries to create a full, accurate and appealing picture of Scalia's originalism.[2]

Scalia's Originalism

Justice Scalia's originalism focuses on the original meaning of the words of the Constitution. More precisely, he advocates textualism, which interprets the Constitution in the same way that one interprets statutes enacted by the legislature.

By adhering to the original meaning of the Constitution, judges are ensuring that the laws which the Founders wrote still mean today what they meant then. Unlike other theories of interpretation, originalism (1) maintains the rule of law by constraining "future decisionmakers so they cannot induce their own personal preferences into the decision; [they] enhance the legitimacy of decisions because they make it clear to the litigants that their case was decided through neutral application of a rule rather than based on a judge's personal preference; and lastly, [they] embolden[s] the decisionmaker to resist the will of a hostile majority" (Kozinski 1589). Moreover, originalism (2) restrains the majority from rewriting laws to reflect their own standards of correctness. Viewing the Constitution as an evolving document that seeks justice and equality is incongruent with the Constitution's purpose. The Constitution is a document for judges to interpret what the law means and not what the law ought to say, and therefore, judges are not in the business of trying to correct society's ills. Scalia's interpretive theory is premised on a hierarchy of interpretation, cited as "text and tradition."[3]

Text

When deciding a case, Scalia first looks at the text, probing for any evidence that there is explicit language that permits or excludes an action. In the lecture series that later became the groundwork for the book "A Matter of Interpretation," Scalia says, "Words have a limited range of meaning and no interpretation that goes beyond that range is permissible" (Scalia 1997: 24). Scalia notes that if someone speaks of using "tacks, staples, screws, nails, rivets, and other things, the general term 'other things' surely refers to other fasteners" (Scalia 1997: 26). Therefore, the *first principle* of originalism is that words must be interpreted commonsensically. So, glue and tape could reasonably be included in the "fasteners" category, but chewing gum could not although it has a sticky makeup. Originalism's *second principle* is that a judge should interpret the words as they would have been interpreted at the time that the Constitution or a statute was written. For example, a judge in the early twentieth century might have been confronted by a group of women claiming that not having the right to vote was against their equal rights as American citizens. If that judge followed originalism, says Scalia, he would have to dismiss the suit because giving women the right to vote was not the original meaning behind the enactment of the Fourteenth Amendment, which contains the Due Process and Equal Protection clauses.

Tradition

Interpreting the Constitution based on the explicit words of the text is fairly straightforward. The procedure behind interpreting the Constitution becomes trickier when the language of the Constitution or a statue is vague. When dissenting in the 1990 case *Rutan v. Republican Party*—in which the Court held that political patronage violates the free speech rights of public employees—Scalia's sardonically noted:

> The provisions of the Bill of Rights were designed to restrain transient majorities from impairing long-recognized personal liberties. . . . Thus, **when a practice not expressly prohibited by the text of the Bill of Rights bears the endorsement of a long tradition of open, widespread, and unchallenged use that dates back to the beginning of the Republic, we have no proper basis for striking it down**.[4] Such a venerable and accepted tradition is not to be laid on the examining table and scrutinized for its conformity to some abstract principle of First Amendment adjudication devised by this Court. . . . When it appears that the latest "rule," or "three-part test," or "balancing test" devised by the Court has placed us on a collision course with such a landmark practice, it is the former that must be recalculated by us, and not the latter that must be abandoned by our citizens.[5]

If the explicit meaning of the Constitution or statue cannot be found Scalia then seeks to interpret the law in this second way using historical context. Justice Scalia's explication of this method is murky. He has said that it is "exceedingly difficult to plumb the original understanding of an ancient text"[6] and that originalism's principle defect is that "historical research is always difficult and sometimes inconclusive."[7] Nevertheless, I have constructed two methods which I believe are in line with Justice Scalia's method of interpretation based on tradition.[8] Scalia relies on tradition by (1) using past case history (often called precedent) and (2) analyzing the long and enduring social practices of our citizenry.[9] In other words, law should only be overturned if there is evidence that a longstanding tradition does not warrant maintaining. For example, Justice Scalia dissented in the 1996 case *United States v. Virginia*, in which the Court proclaimed that the all male admission policy of the Virginia Military Institute violated the Equal Protection Clause of the Fourteenth Amendment. The role of the Court was to "preserve our society's values regarding (among other things) equal protection, not to revise them."[10] In other words, America's longstanding tradition was to separate men and women in military institutions. The fact that just about every other military institution in the Nation was integrated was not the issue, nor was the issue that the separation of genders implied an inherent inequality.

When Scalia cannot find an answer using the "text and tradition" method there is obviously no law to find. While "new times require new law . . . judges have no authority to pursue those broader purposes or write those new laws" (Scalia 1997: 23). Therefore, issues such as the right to privacy and school prayer are issues that should be decided by the legislature.

Making Law

Justice Scalia maintains that originalism is the only theory of adjudication that ensures judges adjudicate laws fairly, with neutrality, and without influence from personal opinions or ideals. Justice Scalia said during his 1986 confirmation hearings that a "constitution has to have ultimately majoritarian underpinnings. To be sure a constitution is a document that protects against future democratic excesses." In other words, reading more into the Constitution in order to find newer or embedded meanings sully the democratic process and the legitimacy of the Constitution.

Justice Scalia argues that judges, and specifically members of the United States Supreme Court, have been increasingly adjudicating based on their personal ideals in recent years. "What secret knowledge, one must wonder, is breathed into lawyers when they become Justices of this Court, that enables them to discern that a practice which the text of the Constitution does not clearly proscribe, and which our people have regarded as constitutional for 200 years, is in fact unconstitutional?"[11] he said in one opinion.

In Scalia's view, judges have been using judicial review in order to strike down laws they find personally objectionable. "How can a judge have the power to erase a law from the books when he or she was not elected by the people?" Scalia might ask. Ely continues this argument, saying that the policy-making power of representatives, born of the "electoral process" (Ely 1980: 4) was a central tenet of our founding government. Ely retorts: "A body not elected or otherwise politically responsible in any significant way is telling the people's elected representative that they cannot govern as they'd like" (Ely 1980: 5). The judiciary, they say, was not written with the expressed consent to empower citizens. Indeed, Scalia is not arguing that the Constitution cannot be seen as an evolving document, but that "supervision of the evolution" should not be "committed to the Courts."[12]

This paper is not advocating interpreting the Constitution as an evolving document. The words and the meaning of the Constitution remain intact. Justice Scalia assumes that any judge who interprets a law other than by looking at either the original meaning or history is using their own views to change society's standards. I will argue that the Constitution, as a sparsely written document, should be interpreted in order to empower citizens. I will maintain that like another vague document, the Ten Commandments, the American Constitution is more of a guide than a strict rule, and must be interpreted actively. While the legislature is given the lawmaking power under the guidelines of the Constitution, I will finally argue that the judiciary may take this role if the legislature does not carry out its duty.

Scalia argues that by injecting one's own principles into interpreting a law (which inevitably he would say the empowerment principle would do) that a judge is damaging the rule of law, which is defined as giving the government authority to enforce the law in only those areas where there is written or established procedures, such as written law or the amendment process. If judges decide that the rule of law does not apply to them, what should stop a judge from, say, suspending the constitutional right against double jeopardy?

Principalism

I follow in a long line of philosophers whom I call principalists. Most famous for advocating this line of interpretation is Professor Ronald Dworkin, who argued that the Constitution was written as a statement of principles in which successive generations could build a society that protects those principles the Founders envisioned were important to the lasting stability of our nation. Dworkin's moral reading argument states that the Constitution, which is grounded in moral abstract principles, can be applied to concrete cases today through fresh moral judgments. Rather than discovering or inventing a new principle, judges use the moral principles that the Founders originally wrote into the Constitution and apply those doctrines to modern day cases. For example, a judge might ask oneself what principle(s) should be invoked when deciding a case about pornography. Naturally, James Madison never imagined something called the Internet, or some of its content. However, judges can take the new case (involving pornography) and apply the old principles embedded in the Constitution. In this case, a judge would refer to the principle that free speech is guaranteed to all citizens, except for when it causes injury or when the speech is proven to harm or be untrue. Since these abstract principles are generally accepted by all, there is no subjectivity to it, argues Dworkin.

The specific theory of interpretation that I advocate is called empowerment rights. Empowerment rights guarantee each citizen the right to be treated with respect and dignity. It is the responsibility of the government to ensure that citizens are not openly or covertly treated as second class citizens. Empowerment rights seek to guarantee that no person is negatively discriminated[13] against because of a perceived or known difference.[14] The empowerment principle is based on a belief that America is a co-operative venture. It takes an entire citizenry to operate our Republic. It means that our government is more than a representative government. The citizenry plays a role in choosing its leaders, holding them to account, never allowing their individual rights to be violated and standing for election when they believe they can do better running our government. Likewise, the government pledges to refrain from abusing fundamental rights of life, equality and due process, while holding those responsible for abusing rights accountable. In addition, each section of our community uses its talents for the benefit of all members of society. I believe this to be Justice Scalia's ultimate flaw. I see our nation as a co-operative venture, which is premised on the basis that when the majority shows contempt for the needs and prospects of the minority that the legislature, and if necessary, the judiciary, has an obligation to remedy the violation.

I can imagine Justice Scalia responding unfavorably to such an open ended definition describing a judge's role. Yet, this is the only way to give judges latitude for the growth of society, just like the Constitution itself was written.

A Document that Empowers

What are the social and cultural implications of Scalia's originalism? If it were up to Scalia, judges would be prohibited from correcting injustices that are visible in society. The federal government would not be held accountable, through the checks and balance system, to remedy violations of fundamental rights. Finally, laws and practices that are known to be unjust would remain in place, and tacitly, given government approval.

Is this something that the Founders would find acceptable? The Constitution of the United States of America was ratified on September 17, 1787. It included seven highly specific articles and ten more general articles that became known as the Bill of Rights. Unlike other Constitutions,[15] Ulrich K. Preuss argues that the American constitution is seen as a quasi-religious document. "The written text is the solemn expression of the mutual promises and obligations of the citizens" (Preuss 2001: 502). The quasi-biblical standing that the Constitution is afforded gives the Constitution more authority than simply a statute. The American Constitution's moral authority, unlike its British and French equivalents, is embedded in the fact that it is a sacred document. The document is *the* defender of American's fundamental rights.

> The making of the constitution is the act of founding the nation, and whatever purposes, aspirations, hopes, fears, achievements, disappointments, traumas and tragedies of the nation through its eventful history may have occurred or may arise in the future, it is the constitution from which the people will try to extract the rights answers to their questions (Preuss 2001: 503).

To many, the Constitution is the backbone of America. Those who fought for American independence sought to create a society where Americans would have the opportunity to create a life based on dignity and worth. The American Constitution, unlike the French and British constitutions, is a living document of hopes and aspirations. The Constitution gives all Americans the opportunity to actively pursue a life of tranquility and to seek justice when their liberties have been violated. A fixed reading of the Constitution leaves no room for a judge to ensure that the Constitution still empowers its citizens more than 200 years later.

The United States is lucky that women followed Justice Scalia's policy and continued to petition the legislature—for about seventy years—for the right to vote. But, should every person, or group, fight this long for a change in an unjust law, especially when the route that Scalia advocates—the legislature—fails in its duty to address an issue? It seems as if many issues relating to the protection of fundamental American liberties go unanswered by the Congress. Why does one get the impression that Congress never acts on important national issues such as abortion and issues of equality? One theory is that politicians are worried that voting on such salient issues will cost them an election. Another theory is that the Tenth Amendment leaves any powers not delegated to the federal government and not prohibited to the state governments, for the states to carry out (Arthur 1995: 37). Therefore, if *Roe v. Wade* was overturned as a federal law, it would be left to every state to decide how they wanted to regulate or prohibit abortion.

By examining *Miranda v. Arizona,* one realizes that sometimes when it is up to state legislatures to implement non-uniformed policy that a non-uniformed protection of fundamental rights emerges.

Article Five of the Constitution reads:

> No person shall be held to answer for a capital, or otherwise infamous crime, unless on a presentment or indictment of a grand jury. . . , **nor shall be compelled in any criminal case to be a witness against himself, nor be deprived of life, liberty, or property, without due process of law. . . .**

Miranda v. Arizona challenged the law enforcement system in the face of sometimes brutal and criminal interrogation by the police. The Court's decision declared that: suspects do indeed have a right against inhumane interrogation processes; a right to be told that they have a right against self-incrimination—better known as the right to remain silent—and the right to a lawyer. Other cases were used as precedent for *Miranda,* especially *Weems v. United States* (1910), in which the Court said:

> Our contemplation cannot be only of what has been, but of what may be. Under any other rule, a constitution would indeed be as easy of application as it would be deficient in efficacy and power. Its general principles would have little value, and be converted by precedent into impotent and lifeless formulas. Rights declared in words might be lost in reality. And this has been recognized. The meaning and vitality of the Constitution have developed against narrow and restrictive construction.[16]

It is a powerful statement. The Court declared, long before the term judicial activism was conceived, that in the judiciary lays a sacred responsibility—to ensure that the rights guaranteed by the Founders were not misinterpreted in later years through a narrow interpretation of the Constitution. And since the general principles of Article Five were not being adhered to, it fell to the judiciary to ensure that a long-suffering problem was rectified. The Court said that it was aware that interrogations occur in secret, which "results in a gap in our knowledge as to what, in fact, goes on in the interrogation rooms."[17] The Court did not set out to make law. Yet, it did so, without any reservation, to ensure that citizens received the equal due process of the law that they were entitled to receive.

Finally, whether Miranda was guilty of a crime was of little consequence. What was of large consequence, however, was the way suspects, especially poor and minority ones, were continually harassed in interrogations, in an attempt to literally beat out a confession. Justice Scalia might argue, "What is the legislature around if not to decide what laws are not working? Why is the legislature's job if not to make and amend law?" The legislature is our law making body, but when the legislature's idleness contributes to a continual violation of a person's fundamental liberties, the legislature's lawmaking power can be taken by the judiciary.

The next question to ask is, "how can a judge who believes in principalism interpret the Constitution fairly?" The next section will argue that judges should be incapable of finding the original meaning because the Founders wrote the text deliberately vague so as not to restrict the liberties of citizens in either the present or future.

A Vague Document Based on Interpretation

Moves to uncover either the original intent or meaning of the Constitution, says Andreas Teuber of Brandeis University, "are frequently frustrated" (Teuber 1988) not because of a lack of trying on the part of judges, "but because the Framers drafted the text in such a way as to leave little trace of their concrete proposals or substantive intentions." Therefore, any way of interpreting the Constitution will involve a level of subjectivity.

Biblical history states that God handed the Ten Commandments to Moses and told Moses (without any other instruction) that this is the law. These ten rules, much like the ten Bill of Rights, have a mixture of specific and general rules. "Thou shalt remember and keep the Sabbath day holy" is the third commandment. What is the original meaning of such a clause? For that matter, is there an objective meaning for "holy?" And how does one go about keeping it holy? I attend church every week, but let's say I oversleep one week. Have I failed to keep the day holy? What if I kill someone on a Sunday but still attend mass. Have I still kept the day holy? These are ponderous questions, but the point I'm trying to make is two-fold.[18]

First, a general principle leads to an array of interpretations, and while not every interpretation is acceptable, there rarely is one interpretation that can supercede all others. For example, columnist James J. Kilpatrick[19] wrote about different judicial interpretations regarding the Sixth Amendment, which states "In all criminal prosecutions, the accused shall enjoy the right to a speed and public trial. . . . " On November 23, 1977, Jack Humphrey died of a single bullet wound to the head. A grand jury indicted his wife in April 1980 for the murder, and she immediately moved for a preliminary hearing and a motion for a speedy trial. In August 1980, the indictment was dismissed after the state failed to establish probable cause. However, a second indictment for the same charge was issued on March 5, 2004. Humphrey moved for an immediate dismissal based on a violation of her constitutional right to a speedy trial because of several setbacks to her case: two of the state's key witnesses were dead, and the rifle used in the shooting—as well as fourteen other items that were a part of the evidence—had disappeared. Humphrey's motion was originally granted because the delay "had critically prejudiced the defendant's ability to prepare for trial" (Kilpatrick, *Staten Island Advance*, 28 December 2005, p. B 21). However, the decision was overturned by the Wyoming Supreme Court. The court said that the roughly twenty-four years in between both indictments had to be "excluded" from the "speedy" trial required by the Constitution.

Justice Lewis Powell, one of the court's more conservative justices, employed four questions in a similar case that he believed were important to guaranteeing a person was given a speedy trial: How long was the delay? What reason(s) justified the delay? Had the defendant asserted his [or her] right speedily to proceed? Was the delay prejudicial to the defendant? Justice Powell added,

> We cannot definitely say how long [a delay] is too long in a system whose justice is supposed to be swift but deliberate. . . . It is impossible to do more than generalize about when those circumstances exist.

As Justice Powell stated, trying to find the objective original meaning in the speedy trial clause would be incredibly subjective. Justice Powell employed these four questions while another justice might have used a difference method to interpret the meaning of the speedy trial clause. Therefore, it is logical to assume that Justice Scalia would in some way be employing his own value judgments when seeking to find the original meaning of the speedy trial clause.

Second, if God, or even Moses, acting as a sort of legislature, felt the need to make a certain principle more specific, then it would have been done. It is perfectly right for the rule to state, "Thou shalt keep the Sabbath day holy by worshipping God, resting from ordinary work and being mindful of God's teaching." Since no such specific principle was stated, it is plausible to believe that actively interpreting the rule *is* required, and that no one specific interpretation automatically supercedes all others, though we can intelligently believe that some interpretations are simply wrong. Likewise, it is also plausible to believe that the Founders believed that the Constitution would be interpreted to meet the changing standards of successive generations.

Expanding the Empowerment Principle

This paper seeks to go beyond simply critiquing Justice Scalia's originalism. My main concern is not only whether the Founders would have wanted the Constitution to be interpreted in such a matter but also whether originalism is in general a good theory of adjudication. If this article has fulfilled its purpose, the answer to this question is no. But first, a further distinction must be made concerning the empowerment principle. This paper attempted to prove that the empowerment principle is more congruent with what the Founders had hoped to be the Constitution's central purpose. However, another intriguing argument is inherently present in this discussion. Namely, is the empowerment principle a better theory of adjudication because the *results* that come from the principle help make society better? For example, the empowerment principle could have been used to decide *Brown v. Board of Education* in two ways. First, the Court could have decided that that no person should be negatively discriminated against because of a perceived or known difference. Therefore, segregating people based on the known difference of race is unconstitutional. The second way the Court could have decided the case was to reason that the empowerment principle helps to create a better society by ensuring that citizens are not negatively discriminated against.

The second method is worthy of another article, but it is disastrous to my case against Justice Scalia. This paper was written in an attempt to hammer at least one of many nails into Justice Scalia's originalism. The point has not been to argue for a living Constitution, or a belief that judges should ensure that the law evolves with society. Writing this paper was an attempt to argue for a sound and moral theory of constitutional interpretation without arguing for a "Pollyannaish"[20] conception of the Constitution. If this paper has been successful, one should finish reading doubting whether using the original meaning theory of Constitutional interpretation is as objective and free from judicial bias as Justice Scalia argues.

Finally, it is important to our supposition to make a distinction between a meta-principle and a substantive principle since the empowerment law fits well into both.[21] A meta-principle is an abstract rule of conduct while a substantive principle gives directions on how to use the principle. For example, "do unto others as you would want done unto yourself" is a meta-principle while Hammurabi's dictate to take an "eye for an eye" is a substantive principle. This paper goes beyond simply advocating the empowerment law meta-principle, which is described as seeking to protect citizens from being negatively discriminated against even when there is no proscribed prohibition of the act (such as segregation) within the Constitution. The goal of this paper has been to offer an alternative to Justice Scalia's originalism, and therefore provide a substantive claim as well.

The substantive claim, therefore, gives the Supreme Court the latitude to decide when such constitutional violations have occurred. This claim hinges, first, on the belief that most fundamental rights are embedded within the Constitution, and second, that the Supreme Court is the final interpreter of what the Constitution says. If we are trying to remain loyal to the Constitution then we must first show that the empowerment principle is embedded in the Constitution. While it is not explicit within the Constitution—and I suspect would be immediately rejected by Justice Scalia—the empowerment principle is nevertheless rooted in the Constitution. Our nation was formed because our forebears demanded that those in power respect each person's right to life, liberty and representation. When the Founder's pronouncements were scorned, our forebears formed this nation, and implicitly, wrote our laws to ensure that these principles—life, liberty and equal representation—were included in the Constitution. While the *practice* of carrying out these principles has been disregarded throughout our nation's history, the empowerment *principle* has remained embedded in our Constitution. To say that these principles are not embedded in the Constitution because they have not been adhered to is erroneous. These principles have always been present. Our society, however, has offended the Constitution by not adhering to these principles.

By outlining such a distinct definition of the empowerment principle, which guarantees that no person is negatively discriminated, one is susceptible to Scalia's charge that principlalists can use the Court to change law simply when they feel the law permits actions that were once prohibited. If the legislature takes the role of denying persons of a certain right (such as gay marriage) that decision is for the legislature, the Courts and the citizenry to decide (as I stated in footnote fourteen it is up to the legislature to decide who can be discriminated against). This discussion hopes to illustrate that the legislature could, and might in some states, outlaw gay marriage. This issue may come up again in ten years and be overturned. Like slavery, it isn't the principle of equality that has changed, but the legislators and judges, and the way society has practiced implementing the principle (even if at times it is implemented wrongly).

Critiques and Responses

Justice Scalia argues that the reason judges have been allowed to make law without the threat of recourse is because judges are not accountable to any institution. In a way, judges are answerable to the electorate through the confirmation proceedings, as many Republican senators pointed out during the confirmation hearings of Justice Samuel Alito. It is nevertheless true that judges are never again subjected to the scrutiny of the electorate.

Some argue that the broad principles in the Constitution which I have spoken of should not be interpreted in the same fashion as the Ten Commandments. The Constitution was written, after all, by a variety of self-interested and opinionated men, who had different visions for the direction of their new republic. The only way that a working document could be agreed on, especially after the debacle of the Articles of Confederation, was if it contained fairly unspecific decrees.

The point is taken. However, I have a problem with such an argument. Let us first imagine the Constitution as an unspecific document that was written simply as a foundation for the Republic; it is based on compromise with the hope or intention that it will be later amended or changed as time passed. If this is the case, and the Constitution is nothing more than an afterthought rather than an "object of fearful significance and wonder,"[22] then I see no reason to view the Constitution as the foundation of our judicial system. If the founders viewed the document, or at least the Bill of Rights, as a postscript, then the Constitution loses its authority as the bedrock of our judicial framework. Therefore, maintaining fidelity to the document would become secondary, and judges could use the Constitution as one of several paths of interpreting law. However, I do not believe this to be the role of our Constitution.

Finally, one must not make the mistake of believing that this paper is about simply adjudicating based on equality or fairness. The constitution is not pliable in the sense that it can bend in order to ensure that everyone's rights are equal. There is a difference between ensuring natural rights and what I argue: an empowerment of rights. Natural law asserts a law is invalid if it is immoral. Judges may therefore overturn laws they feel are antithetical to this notion. Empowerment laws, however, are concerned with balancing the rights of the individual while also ensuring a level of fidelity to the Constitution. Some have expressed concern that it is not the place of nine individuals to have a monopoly over deciding what constitutes issues of equality. I agree with that sentiment. A judge's role is not to simply adjudicate law based on their conception of equality. For example, a mentally handicapped person is not allowed equal access to a driver's license not because that person is of lesser equal standing but because of other considerations that allow the government to "discriminate" against that person. The point is to affirm that equality under the law does not mean that all persons are treated equally, but that their rights are considered equally. For example, person A could argue that not being allowed to smoke in a public facility that is conducive to smoking (such as a bar) is an act of government discrimination. Even if person A was to cite the Fourteenth Amendment (Due Process and Equal Protection), a judge would still have no basis for overturning the prohibition because there is a difference between being discriminated against and being treated or made to feel like a second class citizen. The implication for this is that a judge is not bound to rule in favor of every party that comes into his or her courtroom claiming to have been discriminated against.

Conclusion

This paper does not apologize for its subjectivity, and neither should judges. While opponents continue to seethe at the audacity of the "Men in Black" who usurp the will of the majority, judges should laugh off such pomposity. The rhetoric that many utter is fused more with hatred of a liberal judiciary than by an allegiance to any objective theory of adjudication, which Justice Scalia eventually argues is not fully attainable (Scalia 1997: 132).[23] Justice

Scalia said, "I am left with a sense of dissatisfaction, as I am sure you are, that a discourse concerning what one would suppose to be rather fundamental—indeed the most fundamental—aspect of constitutional theory and practice should end so inconclusively."[24] One must concede that both sides of the political spectrum are guilty of stacking the courts in the hope of changing the philosophical tide of American thought. This is a problem, however, that will not be solved by arguing that originalism is the best theory of adjudication simply because it is the lesser evil.

Take Justice Scalia's tradition principle, for example. J. M. Balkin argues in "Tradition, Betrayal and the Politics of Deconstruction" that "Justice Scalia's opinion(s) relies upon a distinction between more or less specific traditions ... which is manipulable and difficult to maintain." For example, the 1989 case *Michael H. v. Gerald D.* dealt with the issue of whether to allow visitation rights to a biological father for a child conceived during adultery. Justice Scalia wrote an opinion that held against the biological father, citing the preservation—and the right—of a child to be raised in a "unitary family"[25] and that there is no embedded constitutional right to a parental relationship. This unitary family principle, rather than a model of objectivity, simply beat out the principle that a biological father and his child should have meaningful contact. In other words, Justice Scalia subjectively chose between competing principles. This is hardly the apex of objective jurisprudence.

American jurisprudence will continue to rely on judges to make pivotal decisions in our nation's history. America, as a co-operative venture, would be better served if we were to honestly admit that unfortunately some judges seek to advance a personal agenda. Yet, there is no branch of government that is free of the foibles of fallibility. It impairs democracy when decisions are made for personal or political reasons. Yet, we can be sure that the judicial branch of government is less concerned about opinion polls and re-elections, and therefore, better able to deliberate on how best to end violations of constitutional liberties, because in the end, an overwhelming majority of judges will put their duty toward consistency and integrity before any egregious misinterpretation of the Constitution.

Finally, we can be sure that no person has been *wronged*—though they may have been offended—by the Supreme Court widening our conception of freedom of speech; no person has suffered from more discrimination because the Court has expanded the view of equality, and no person has been wronged by limiting the unchecked power of the government. Yet, we can be sure that many more people, including eight year old Linda Brown, would have been fundamentally wronged if *Brown* and other cases had not been legislated from the bench. The sting of originalism would, indeed, be too much to bear.

Notes

1 There is still disagreement over whether Chief Justice John Roberts and Justice Samuel Alito fall into this theory of constitutional interpretation.

2 My construction of Justice Scalia's originalism is based on his speeches and on commentary by others, though there will be debate over whether these can be described as scholarly works.

3 There are several sources for this phrase, though, to my knowledge, it has never been uttered by Scalia himself.

4 Emphasis added.

5 Ralph A. Rossum, "The Wit and Wisdom of Justice Scalia," (Sept. 2005). The Claremont Institute. 22 February 2006, http://www.claremont.org/writings/crb/summer 2005/rossum.html.

6 Justice Antonin Scalia, "The Lesser Evil," *University of Chicago Law Review*. 22 February 2006, Reprinted with permission at http://www.joink.com/homes/users/ninoville/lesserevil.asp.

7 Ibid.

8 Special thanks to Steven P. Scalet, Ph.D. for helping me fully explicate a theory of interpretation based on "tradition."

9 In the forthcoming cited excerpt, Scalia uses the word "our" to describe society. I take this to mean our collective society throughout the ages and not our society in the present. The latter interpretation goes against Scalia's main premise.

10 Justice Antonin Scalia, Cornell Law School Legal Law Institute, (Dissent) United States v. Virginia et al., (1996). 22 February 2006, http://www.law.cornell.edu/supct/search/display.html?terms=Virginia%20Military%20Institute&url=/supct/html/94-1941.ZS.html.

11 Justice Antonin Scalia, Cornell Law School Legal Law Institute, (Dissent) *O'Hare Truck Service, Inc. v. City of Northlake* 518 U.S. 712 (1996). 22 February 2006, http://www.law.cornell.edu/supct/html/95-191.ZD.html.

12 Justice Antonin Scalia, "The Lesser Evil," *University of Chicago Law Review*. 22 February 2006, Reprinted with permission at http://www.joink.com/homes/users/ninoville/lesserevil.asp.

13 Special thanks to Professor Scalet who pointed out that professors positively discriminate good papers from bad papers all the time.

14 The fundamental point here is not the definition. I am aware that a polygamist, for example, could use this definition to claim that he/she was being discriminated against. It is within the legislature's duty to refine this definition and list specific groups in society who can be discriminated against.

15 In the interest of space I have removed a discussion about the British and French constitutions, which have historically been secondary documents in comparison to the legislature. In other words, the authority of their constitutions has come from what powers the legislatures have put into the Constitution. Rather, in the United States, it is the Constitution which has given authority to the legislature.

16 Chief Justice Earl Warren, Cornell Law School Legal Law Institute, (Opinion) *Miranda v. Arizona* 384 U.S. 436 (1966). 22 February 2006, http://www.law. cornell.edu/supct/html/historics/USSC_CR_0384_0436_ZO.html.

17 Chief Justice Earl Warren, Cornell Law School Legal Law Institute, (Opinion) *Miranda v. Arizona* 384 U.S. 436 (1966). 22 February 2006, http://www.law. cornell.edu/supct/html/historics/USSC_CR_0384_0436_ZO.html.

18 Part of this argument is also expressed in Professor Teuber's paper, although this argument was conceived before reading his argument, and therefore was not pilfered from him.

19 From his 28 December 2005 column, "Covering the Courts."

20 This seems to be one of Justice Scalia's favorite words and is used often.

21 Thanks to Professor Scalet for his helpful insight.

22 Gordon S. Wood, "Comment" in *A Matter of Interpretation: Federal Courts and the Law,* Antonin Scalia (Princeton University Press, 1997), 62.

23 Paradoxically, there are more "conservative" local and federal judges (included Supreme Court justices) in this country than "liberal" judges.

24 Justice Antonin Scalia, "The Lesser Evil," *University of Chicago Law Review*. 22 February 2006, Reprinted with permission at http://www.joinkcom/homes/users/ ninoville/lesserevil.asp.

25 J. M. Balkin, "Tradition, Betrayal, and the Politics of Deconstruction," (1998). 1 March 2006, http://www.yale.edu/lawweb/jbalkin/articles/trad1.htm.

Works Cited

Arthur, John. (1995). *Words that Bind.* Boulder: Westview Press.

Balkin, J. M. (1998). "Tradition, Betrayal, and the Politics of Deconstruction." 1 March 2006, http://www.yale.edu/lawweb/jbalkin/articles/trad1.htm.

Dworkin, Ronald. (1986). *Law's Empire.* Cambridge: The Belknap Press.

Hart, John Ely. (1980). *Democracy and Distrust: A Theory of Judicial Review.* Cambridge and London: Harvard University Press.

Kozinski, Alex. (1990). "My Pizza with Nino." *Cardozo Law Review* 12: 1583–1591.

Levin, Mark R. (2005). *Men in Black: How the Supreme Court is Destroying America.* Washington, DC: Regency Publishing, Inc.

Miranda v. Arizona, 384 U.S. 436 (1965), Cornell University Law School Legal Information Institute.

Post, Robert. (1990). "Theories of Interpretation." *Representations* (Spring).

Preuss, Ulrich K. (2001). "The Political Meaning of Constitutionalism: British, French and American Perspectives," in John Arthur and William H. Shaw (3rd ed.), *Readings in the Philosophy of Law.* Upper Saddle River: Prentice Hall, pp. 496–506.

Justice Antonin Scalia. (2005). "A Theory of Constitutional Interpretation, 1996, Nino-Ville." 30 Nov. http://www.joink.com/homes/users/ninoville/cua10-18-96.asp.

Justice Antonin Scalia. (2005). "Constitutional Interpretation the Old Fashion Way," 14 March 2005. The Center for Individual Freedom, 20 January, http://www.cfif.org/htdocs/freedomline/current/guest_commentary/scalia-constitutional-speech.htm.

Scalia, Justice Antonin. (1997). *A Matter of Interpretation: Federal Courts and the Law.* Princeton: Princeton University Press.

Teuber, Andreas. (1998). "Original Intent or How Does the Constitution Mean?" *The London Review of Books* (March). 16 Dec. 2005, http://people.brandeis.edu/~teuber/originalintent.html.

Weaver, Jace. (1993). *Then to the Rock Let Me Fly: Luther Bohanon and Judicial Activism.* Norman and London: University of Oklahoma Press.

ABOUT THE CONTRIBUTORS

Stephanie A. Dodge received her Bachelor's Degree in Philosophy, Politics and Law from Binghamton University in the spring of 2006, where she graduated Cum Laude with departmental honors. She is currently a Juris Doctor candidate at St. John's University School of Law, and she is expected to graduate in the spring of 2009. She is on the Executive Board of the Student Bar Association, and she is the Research & Symposium Editor of the St. John's Journal of Legal Commentary. Her current research includes further studies into violence against women, and her latest piece is titled, "Domestic Violence in an Adversarial System: Leveling the Playing Field in Custody Disputes," which was submitted to the St. John's Journal of Legal Commentary for publication.

Angela Godhwani, Binghamton University, class of 2006, is an alumna of the Harpur College of Arts and Sciences. She graduated with departmental honors and earned her Bachelor's Degree in Philosophy, Politics and Law, and simultaneously in English, with a Rhetoric-concentration. Angela is currently pursuing a Master's Degree at Cornell University in Industrial Labor Relations, with concentrations in Human Resources and Organizations, and International and Comparative Labor. Her anticipated graduation date is January 2010.

Sari Goldmeer, a 2004 summa cum laude graduate of Binghamton University, received her Bachelor of Arts in Philosophy, Politics and Law. She went on to receive her Masters Degree in Library and Information Science.

Sari is now working as a High School Library Media Specialist in Westchester County helping to prepare students for post-secondary research endeavors.

Remington A. Gregg graduated with honors from Binghamton University in 2006 (*magna cum laude* and Phi Beta Kappa) with a degree in Philosophy, Politics and Law. He worked in field organizing before entering New York Law School (J.D. candidate, 2010). He remains active in the study of originalism as it gains greater acceptance in mainstream jurisprudence, and plans to publish more on issues related to constitutional interpretation. His other areas of scholarship keep him busy as a Peer Instructor, member of the school's Faculty Selection Committee and Justice Action Center, and as a Research Assistant to Nadine Strossen, Professor of Law and President of the American Civil Liberties Union (ACLU).